SEVEN GUITARS

1948

THE AUGUST WILSON CENTURY CYCLE

SEVEN GUITARS

1948

AUGUST WILSON

FOREWORD BY TONY KUSHNER

THEATRE COMMUNICATIONS GROUP
NEW YORK
2007

The August Wilson Century Cycle is published by Theatre Communications Group, Inc.,
520 Eighth Avenue, 24th Floor, New York, NY 10018-4156

The August Wilson Century Cycle is funded in part by the Ford Foundation, with addi-
tional support from The Paul G. Allen Family Foundation, The Heinz Endowments
and the New York State Council on the Arts.

TCG books are exclusively distributed to the book trade by Consortium Book Sales
and Distribution, 1045 Westgate Drive, St. Paul, MN 55114.

LIBRARY OF CONGRESS CATALOGING-IN-PUBLICATION DATA
Wilson, August.
Seven guitars / August Wilson ; foreword by Tony Kushner.—1st ed.
p. cm.—(August Wilson century cycle)
ISBN 978-1-55936-301-3
1. African Americans—Drama. 2. Blues musicians—Drama. 3. Pittsburgh (Pa.)—
Drama. I. Title.
PS3573.I45677S48   2007
812'.54—dc22   2007022278

Text design and composition by Lisa Govan
Slipcase and cover design by John Gall
Cover photograph by Wayne Miller/Magnum Photos
Slipcase photographs by Dana Lixenberg (author) and David Cooper

First Edition, September 2007

For my wife,
Constanza Romero,
without whom my life would lack
the occasion of poetry
that her presence demands

FOREWORD

by Tony Kushner

WHY SEVEN GUITARS? Only two make their appearance on stage during the play: the old acoustic guitar Floyd is stuck with after the electric guitar he's pawned proves to be irretrievable, and the guitar that Floyd, suddenly, mysteriously flush, purchases before his triumphal gig at the Blue Goose, "the same kind of guitar as Muddy Waters got . . ." Even if we count the offstage pawned electric guitar, yearned after and then unceremoniously abandoned to the pawnbroker in favor of something newer, we're still four guitars short.

There isn't a simple, certain explanation of the title, which makes it altogether appropriate for this vast, troubled, complicated drama. *Seven Guitars*, play number five, marks the midpoint in August Wilson's cycle, and in the century that is the cycle's temporal setting and subject. It's very much a play about time, which is consistently returned to as a topic for discussion among its characters.

Seven Guitars is set in 1948, forty-four years after the cycle began with *Gem of the Ocean*, eight-five years after the Emancipation Proclamation, three or four hundred years into the

African Diaspora, eighty-three years since the Thirteenth Amendment, halfway into the twentieth century, and surely the curtain should be rising on progress, on social transformation. Justice should have arrived by now, after so much time, so much suffering, so much oppression and so much blood; however imperfect, some clear sign of steady progress toward social, racial, political, economic justice should have arrived. But eighty-three years after the abolition of slavery ushered in Jim Crow, fifty-two years after *Plessy v. Ferguson*, radical transformation is not yet palpable nor discernibly immanent in the Hill District, in postwar, economically depressed, racist America. The play is about knowing and not knowing what time it is, about time passing, but even more significantly, about time stalling, with tragic consequence.

Because my memories of the original production of *Seven Guitars* are so vivid, I was shocked to realize that it opened on Broadway way back in 1996. It's very rare that a play gets a perfect cast, but *Seven Guitars* had one, seven gorgeous performances (theatrically and, where required, musically!), each actor so precisely creating his or her character that it's unimaginable that August Wilson didn't write the parts for them, whether or not he actually did. The late great Lloyd Richards directed it, as he had directed the previous cycle plays, with thrilling confidence in the play, the cast and the audience. Richards's restraint beautifully matched Wilson's unique version of realism. The story was allowed to proceed digressively, discursively, at an unhurried tempo, until the tensions building up underneath the daringly undramatic surface exploded with terrifying power.

But as I watched the play for the first time, I was most struck by what I understood to be its delineation, through an interweaving of politics, psychology and theology, of the costly agony for individuals and for communities waiting for the messiah, desperately in need of and trying to survive the wait for a savior, a promised one who will redeem time, bring justice, resurrect the dead.

Doesn't all great drama include God in the debate? Don't all great playwrights grapple with theological questions that thread through human affairs? Eugene O'Neill, the playwright August Wilson most resembles, did that. Even an atheist like Brecht did it. The plays of Wilson's cycle most emphatically do, and none of his plays more emphatically, I think, than this one. Most of the plays in the cycle address the conflicts between fathers and sons: the grief-stricken disappointment sons feel in fathers who are incapable of saving them; the disrespect and abuse those disappointed sons direct at their beaten-down fathers; the violent anger the wounded, humiliated fathers visit upon their offspring. In *Seven Guitars* this mutual dependence, tearing, incomprehension, guilt and anger are constants not only among the generations of men, loving and resenting, wanting to be saviors, waiting to be saved, but a central aspect of the relationship between the human and the divine.

The play isn't a religious allegory with a neatly labeled messiah, but rather the depiction of a world of thwarted expectation, suffused with various kinds of messianism. A host of salvational figures swim in and out of view. There's the gigantic, hovering presence of heavyweight champion Joe Louis, paragon, exemplar, deliverer of pride to the African-American community. There are saviors long-dead yet still long-anticipated, figures from black history who brought redemption and liberation, of however limited a scope: Marcus Garvey, Toussaint-Louverture, and, most strangely and most hauntingly, the quasi-mythical progenitor of jazz, the cornetist Buddy Bolden.

The protagonist of *Seven Guitars*, the tragic central focus of its messianism, is Floyd "Schoolboy" Barton. Floyd is not a shepherd—this isn't a pastoral world, as the fate of Miss Tillery's poor rooster makes clear—but rather the leader of a band, and thus a man with pastoral responsibilities, who is, as

Red Carter says, "supposed to take care" of the other musicians. Floyd's talent, sexuality, celebrity and his raging dignity
draw others to him and to his promise of transcendence, joy, a
better world to come in Chicago. According to Vera, his funeral
and grave site are attended by angels, in whose company, after
death, conquering death, he ascends.

His miraculous gift is music, which may bring the money
everyone in the play is lacking. Music may even bring back the
dead, or at least it almost seems to when Floyd sings his mother's
version of The Lord's Prayer. It's the "almost" that's the problem.

Floyd demands of himself and of those whom he would
have follow him, Vera and his band members, something harder
than the incredibly difficult faith Jesus demanded of the apostles. Floyd demands belief in self-reliance, merit and the value
of striving, in making justice manifest through a determined
exertion of talent, wit, courage and will, and he insists on this
with persuasive assurance, in spite of the fact that, as he also
insists on telling his followers, everywhere he turns he encoun-
ters the indignities, traps, moral, physical and spiritual injuries
of what James Baldwin called the "mangling machinery of
racism." Floyd's life is proof of the futility of his belief. His
faith is in a providence he *almost* knows is a phantasm.

And not just Floyd's faith. Vera must believe in Floyd,
who has deceived her before and who will, she knows, deceive
her, and himself, again and again. Nevertheless, Vera believes,
or tries to. She says of Floyd's Chicago, his gospel's heaven, "the
way he talk about it do make you want to see it . . . Maybe I can
be a different person up there."

This contingent, delusional almost-gospel would have
been familiar to O'Neill's characters, it's what keeps the
denizens of Harry Hope's bar in *The Iceman Cometh* alive.
Among the drunks in *Iceman*, the addiction to groundless hope
is ultimately meant to be understood as ahistorical and
inescapable, an essential aspect of existence common to all
humanity; the impaupered rummies and their desolate bar are

more metaphoric than historic. In *Seven Guitars*, the need to cling to illusion derives not from some immutable, existential flaw in humanity, but from bloody history and a malevolent politics, the consequence of malign human agency, of The Dream Deferred.

Poverty, vagrancy laws, police brutality, kangaroo courts, catch-22 business contracts and insurance swindles have intruded too strongly on Floyd's soul to permit any faith more substantial than a tormented, taunting agnosticism, or rather a Manichean gnosticism, with the world starkly split in two by race, with God largely absent and the devil filling in. For all of his talent, galvanic attractiveness, gravity, incandescence, for all that the play and the other characters' expectations position him as hero, Floyd is heartbreakingly unable to locate within himself the heroic self-knowledge that he knows is fundamental to acquiring power and meaning in the world. "I don't know what you all think of yourself, but I think I'm supposed to have . . . Have something. Have anything." His fiercely enterprising, indomitable spirit, at a moment of truth, reveals as its hypostasis a shaky speculation, riven with uncertainty. It's as much a question as an assertion: He *thinks* he's supposed to have. Something? Anything?

Floyd's tenuous, self-canceling faith is set in sharp contrast to the unshakeable visionary certitude of King Hedley. Even though Hedley seems to have lost the ability to distinguish between reality and his messiah-agitated imagination, Floyd knows that Hedley's dreams have given him the nearest thing anyone in the play possesses to confident belief. In a mad world, it may be madness that's the key to clarity. "If he don't know the consequences," Floyd says of Hedley, "he's gonna find out the truth. Hedley know who he is. He know what he think of himself." Floyd's life is crushing his faith, his certainty, but Hedley *knows*. Floyd knows the consequences too well; not knowing the consequences has helped crazy Hedley know the Truth. He doesn't know who's fathered Ruby's child, but he knows whose Child Ruby's baby will be, and *who* he will be: a black man, a King, a Lion of Judah, perhaps, according to Hedley's paraphrasing of Psalm 68, the Prince promised to come forth after "Ethiopia stretches forth her wings."

Floyd, who was parented by his mother, doesn't talk about his earthly father, and he appears to be trapped in a maternal drama of unsuccessful individuation and separation, replayed in his adult life as serial abandonment of and by women, the faithful Vera and the unfaithful Pearl. His mother, whom Floyd clearly adored, will get her headstone from her son, and then Floyd will leave her town, and her, behind him. "I get her that marker," he declares, "and I won't owe nobody nothing." Perhaps Wilson means us to understand that because of his lack of paternity, fatherless Floyd is blinded by an illusion of disconnectedness masquerading as freedom. Floyd's opposite, again, is Hedley, who has had a father to contend with. Torturous as the contention has been, it has indebted Hedley, and thus it's rooted him. Hedley knows he has to struggle to forgive his father his helplessness and his violence, and to ask his father's forgiveness for his son's reproaches, for his tongue. This is both psychological reconciliation and a formula for prayer, for appeasing fathers and The Father—on earth, in the psyche, or on the Throne of Heaven. The struggle reconciles divided sons to the long waiting for deliverance, and prepares them for the task of making and raising sons of their own and, maybe, The Son. Hedley believes he could be the father of the messiah.

Hedley's faith, original and jumbled as it appears to be, is the faith of his fathers, or rather faith *in* his fathers, incorporating nineteenth-century Ethiopianism, Garveyism and Haitian slave revolts, as well as his flesh-and-blood father's history. Spectral Buddy Bolden, whose biography is sketchy, derived from anecdote, who spent his last twenty-four years in a mental hospital, whose grave is unknown, whose few recordings have been swallowed up by time, is ideally suited, by virtue of the mythifying mystery in which his life is shrouded, to his transfiguration as Hedley's deliverer. Floyd adds, concluding his admiration of Hedley, "And he know what he think of the white man." Floyd sounds envious of Hedley's Afrocentrist cosmology, a part of his paternal inheritance, which serves to fortify and protect him, as it has generations before him. Hedley's crazy but in this, too, he sees more clearly than Floyd, who has been given more than enough painful information to know what to expect of white people, but whose impatience and anger reveal a refusal, an incapacity to be disillusioned, and whose desires lead him back, repeatedly, to confront dangerous irreconcilables, to have historically impossible expectations.

Hedley is older than Floyd, and his faith is old. Floyd is younger, and attracted, arguably fatally, to modernity, motion, emigration and progress. The gun is superior to the knife, he argues, and an electric guitar to an acoustic guitar, and anonymous migrant-filled Chicago to stagnant Pittsburgh. The recently invented atomic bomb trumps them all (as, indeed, Death does). Knowing the time is critical in *Seven Guitars*. Floyd arrives to embrace the New before the New is available and willing to be embraced. This is fruitful (Floyd has had a hit record, albeit one from which he's derived no profit), and catastrophic.

With their merely exclusive identification of men and paternity as the arena within which historical agency unfolds, with their insistent depiction of women as mothers and nurturers, Wilson's plays have been called patriarchal and conservative. Whatever else might be at work, Wilson's particular fabulations of an African-American spiritual/political organicity is recognizably a strategy of resistance to the social disintegration and death of slavery, segregation, and persistent, pervasive, virulent racism. As all strategies are, this one is limited and problematic; but if August Wilson, as he exists in his plays, can be called a patriarchal conservative, he isn't a dogmatist or an ideologue. He is, he was, a dramatist, which is to say a dialectitian. He offers us the means of recognizing in tribalism and separatism both radical and reactionary impulses, both strategies for survival and risky paranoid delusion. He gives us female characters, and male as well, who chafe and bridle at their roles within traditions of gender. He neither fetishizes, mechanizes nor demonizes progress. His characters grapple with the retrograde motion of change, inevitable and ineluctable. Consonant or dissonant, they face the abrasions of progress and pay the price, and watching them we learn about the role these opposite attitudes toward progress play in individual and social vitality. Both conservatism and progressivism, reflective or not of Wilson's personality and politics, are embodied full-bloodedly, dialectically in his plays, in his characters and their dramatic, occasionally tragic conflicts.

The first tragic climax of the collision between Hedley's certainty and the jittery new gospel of which Floyd is avatar carries off Miss Tillery's rooster—an Alabama rooster who, like all of his breed, according to the magnificently informed and informative Canewell, doesn't know what time it is, and dies, in Hedley's hands, for the sin. It's a breathtaking moment, revealing behind Hedley's patriarchal, conservative coherence a frightening, repressed violence and chaos. It's also a gesture and image of pure poetry, this prophet murdering an annunciatory angel, whose cry, "Wake up!" echoes Floyd's recurrent line in his ongoing theological debate with Hedley.

The debate takes the form of the disputed lyric of the song "I Thought I Heard Buddy Bolden Say." Over and over, Hedley prophetically tries to deliver the news, the gospel, to a waiting world, singing, "I thought I heard Buddy Bolden say . . ." What comes next is the question.

FLOYD: He said, "Wake up and give me the money."
HEDLEY: Naw. Naw. He say, "Come here. Here go the money."

Floyd's answer, his gospel, sounds like a simple strong command, direct, active, peremptory even, but clear as day. Hedley's is grammatically odd, disturbingly vague: Is Buddy Bolden saying, "If you come to me, I will give you your reward."? Or is it a bait and switch, a come and go? "You come here, while—whoops!—the money's going elsewhere." In these two lines, the difference between the two men, one active and impatient, the other dreamily adrift, appears to have been starkly defined.

But Floyd's line only sounds clear at first hearing. If it's Buddy Bolden saying, "Wake up," to whom is he speaking? Whoever it is that's being told to wake up is the same person of whom it is demanded, "give me the money." So who is demanding awakedness of whom, and who is demanding a rendering? If Bolden is waking up Floyd, Hedley, and us, in which direction is the money going to flow?

Hedley's version of the lyric reminds me of Wallace Stevens's "The honey of heaven may or may not come / But that of earth both comes and goes at once." For black people, in 1948, for the characters of *Seven Guitars*, most of them losing as fast as they can manage any gain, Hedley's line is less a poetical paradox than a blunt description of an ugly, unendurable reality.

What initially makes these two men seem unalike begins to lose its distinctness. Floyd *thinks* he knows who he is, and Hedley *thought* he heard Buddy Bolden say . . . something. Floyd's gospel is action, a demand for progress, and Hedley's is distrust in progress and a reconciliation, if not resignation, to waiting; but theirs is a shared rejection of injustice, a shared passion for justice, and, as time will reveal, a shared despair produced by ceaseless disappointment, protraction, thwarting. Neither Hedley's certainty nor Floyd's uncertainty spares either man from an excruciating posture of expectation, from hope which becomes, through ceaseless delay, unnerving, demoralizing and debilitating. When Floyd asks Hedley what

Buddy Bolden has given him, or will give him, Hedley responds surprisingly: "Ashes." Not money, or a plantation, as he's been declaring he'll get since the play began, but merely a version of the "something, anything" Floyd thinks he's meant to have.

(Though the actual words of "I Thought I Heard Buddy Bolden Say" are lost, apparently it wasn't a song about riches but bodily smells. "I thought I heard Buddy Bolden say / 'Funky-butt, funky-butt, take it away . . .'" So the line Floyd and Hedley argue over isn't about gold, but shit; shit, or ashes, for that matter, and filthy lucre amounting, according to skeptical, psychoanalytic and moral readings of value, to the same thing.)

When Hedley kills the rooster, he tells the others that "God ain't making no more roosters. It is a thing past. Soon you mark my words when God ain't making no more niggers. They too be a done thing." On one hand, this declaration may be redemptive, if "nigger" is read or heard as "craven, corrupt," distinct from the proud black man Hedley insists he is or aspires to become; but it's just as easily understood equating roosters and all black people and prophesying doom for both. In either reading, Hedley's meaning is unignorable: destruction, extinction, extermination are preludes to future time. The obverse of Hedley's organic, rooted coherence is murderous madness, and the vision shadowing his upbeat insistence on God's munificence and beneficence is the Apocalypse.

The rooster announces the arrival of a messiah, Floyd; and Hedley is the prophet of the messiah, he's Elijah, he's John the Baptist. But it's his belief that he may be losing Ruby to Floyd that catalyzes Hedley's recognition that Floyd is "like a king!" In *Seven Guitars*, jealousy, rivalry, murderous hate, rather than ecstasy, reveal the Anointed to his Prophet. When finally, fatally, Floyd in Hedley's eyes becomes Buddy Bolden himself, becomes the earthly incarnation of a God who permits his children to endure evil without end, Hedley kills the King. Floyd's last words are, "I'll see you tomorrow." Hedley's tired of waiting for tomorrow, tired of waiting for the promised deliverance. "This time, Buddy," he says, bloody machete in his hands, "you give me the money."

At the end of the play, that goddamned money, the killing promise everyone's been waiting for, falls "to the ground like ashes."

So why *seven* guitars? The number seven recurs in the play at various points. There are seven characters. Red Carter had seven women, one for each day of the week, and he sees seven birds sitting on the backyard fence. Floyd says that he once had "seven ways to go" before these were taken away, one by one, as his life is systematically whittled down, from amplitude to unyielding, hardscrabble scarcity, to "living without." Floyd is a musician. Is each of these "ways to go" figured in a guitar?*

There's no correct answer to the title's numerological mystery, there's only an invitation to wonder. Since one of my favorite films is Ingmar Bergman's *The Seventh Seal*, and since, it seems to me, Apocalypse figures large in the imaginations of the characters of *Seven Guitars*, the title has a Book-of-Revelation ring in my ears. In Revelation there are lots of number sevens: seven stars, seven golden candlesticks, seven churches which are in Asia, seven spirits which are before the Throne of God. Most famously, there's a book, fastened with seven seals, which is held by the awesome figure seated on God's right hand, descendant of David, the risen Messiah.

---

*Another seven, having to do with time: the Joe Louis–Billy Conn boxing match actually took place in 1941, seven years before the play begins. I've interviewed several people who worked with Wilson on the original production, all of whom agree that he was aware of the anachronism; the high stakes and terrific drama of the Conn fight, when Louis was in his prime, fighting against a white opponent, suited the playwright's purposes better than the Brown Bomber's only major 1948 fight, against Jersey Joe Walcott, in which both contestants were black and battling middle-age as much as one another. Wilson felt the misdating was covered by dramatic and poetic license.

When he opens the seventh seal, there will be a silence in heaven, and then . . .

Is *Seven Guitars* an apocalypse? Is this play, only halfway through the cycle's story, in which the deliverer comes and is murdered by one who hopes for deliverance, meant as an impatient, despairing anticipation of the end of everything, or an almost end? Is there silence after the seventh guitar?

There's one other number seven in the play. Hedley, lost in his dreams, waving his machete, tells Ruby, "I offer you a kingdom . . . the flesh of my flesh, my seven generations . . ." Hedley offers no explanation of what he means by that. I will hazard a guess. In the Gospel according to Luke, there are seventy-seven generations in Jesus' genealogy, connecting Adam in the Garden to the baby in the manger in Bethlehem. And every seventh generation along the way to Jesus, as Luke has arranged it, a significant figure appears, including King David. Are Hedley's seven generations an installation in the progress toward the Second Coming? Is he the endpoint of a set of seven generations, or its inceptor?

Adam's genealogy begins in the Torah, in the Hebrew Bible, in Genesis. The first significant counting of seven generations, however, doesn't begin with Adam, but with his son Cain. In the seventh generation descended from Cain, Lamech, Cain's great-great-great-great grandson, fathers three boys, Jabal, Jubal and Tubal-Cain. Jabal, the eldest, is a shepherd, like his murdered great-great-great-great-great uncle Abel. The other two boys of Cain's seventh generation are workers of implements and instruments, like their fratricidal ancestor. Jubal invents musical instruments. Tubal-Cain develops metallurgy and the forging of weapons.

Musical instruments and weapons are conjoined in Genesis as they are in *Seven Guitars*, with its knives, guns, guitars, harmonicas and drums. There is, in the play, a proximity, an intimate connection between music and violence, and in history as well. It's to be found in this a passage from the jazz saxophonist Sidney Bechet's autobiography, *Treat It Gentle*:

> The police would come by sometimes and, like I say, some of them didn't do nothing to stop what was going on, but others used to beat up the people and break them up and get them moving away from there . . . Once, I remember, Buddy Bolden was out there singing and playing . . . a song of his that got to be real famous, "I Thought I Heard Buddy Bolden Say." The words to that, they wasn't considered too nice. A lot of mothers would hear their kids singing [it] when they came home . . . and if the kids were scratched up at all, or hurt some, the mothers they'd know right away where their kids had been, because as often as not someone did get scratched up when they hung around listening . . .

Is Hedley's invocation of "seven generations" meant to allude to this conjoining of hope (music) and despair (violence), a fusion of messianism with the story of Cain and Abel, with fratricide? Floyd's murder at Hedley's hands is in one sense parricide, regicide, deicide, a despairing refusal to wait any longer for God's arrival, a lashing out at God, when he arrives, for having made the wait so monstrously long. In another sense, it is caused by sexual rivalry and jealousy, and is as old, ordinary and horrible as brother killing brother.

God marks Cain to warn others that anyone who harms Cain will suffer punishment unto his (the assailant's) seventh generation. But as Lamech, who fathers Cain's seventh generation of descendants, understands God's marking, Cain's murder itself will take seven generations to have been avenged. Lamech, who has been guilty of injuring a man and a child, speculates that if seven generations were necessary for justice following the murder of Abel, seventy-seven generations will have to pass before his own crime has been avenged. Is this the source of Luke's seventy-seven generations? Seven, at any rate, is the number of both vengeance and redemptive absolution.

Jewish tradition recounts tales of Moshiach arriving but, dissatisfied with the welcome, or the readiness of people to enter the New Time his arrival is meant to inaugurate, he departs again, leaving the world broken as before. These traditions warn of the necessity of readiness, of not being overly attached to the familiar and the habitual, and warning also that since any stranger might be Moshiach, finally arrived, all strangers must be treated as if they were Moshiach. The Christian Messiah comes to earth, heals the sick, embraces the sinful, preaches peace and a rejection of material things, and is tortured and savagely murdered by the heedless officials and soldiers of a cruel and mighty empire, who have no idea who they're killing.

The savior, the redeemer, the deliverer of the world from political evil or from fallen grace, or both, may be false or true, may come and go, may vanish or bleed to death, and then . . . The apostles wait.

Midway through the play, when Hedley and Floyd discuss the resurrection of the dead through music, Hedley says, about his dead grandmother, "I used to sit and play and try to hear her. Once. Maybe. Almost." Those three words describe the agonized, longing and scorched heart of *Seven Guitars*. Once. Maybe. Almost.

Messianism, Jewish or Christian, is teleological, posits a narrative with a beginning and an end. People suffer, the King arrives, and time ends. But it's never quite so simple. In Jewish tradition, Moshiach makes repeated appearances and disappearances. In Jewish history, messiahs have appeared, partially succeeding or entirely failing to inaugurate a New Time. In Christianity, Jesus arrives to fulfill the messianic promises of Jewish Scripture, which doesn't mention that the Heir of the Throne of Jesse and the House of David will be arrested, brutalized and slaughtered; or that humankind, having failed its King, will have to await, for an unspecified time, a Second Coming. Christianity too, has its history of failed and false Returns. While these reversals, disappointments and complications are incorporated into doctrine, traces of unsettled unreliability, infusions of doubt, linger to disturb orthodoxy's convictions. Within the expectant narratives of teleological faiths, remnants are discerned of something cyclical, the singing of an earlier song, in which vengeance and defeat accompany redemption, in which a nonlinear, paradoxical simultaneity of defeat and redemption is revealed. Death and birth (or rebirth) occupy the same space, the same moment in time. Shadowing triumph, there is tragedy. In August Wilson's cycle, as in his dramatic antecedents, in the earliest dramatic cycles, there is forward motion, but there is also the cyclical.

August Wilson's cycle is constructed on a foundation of clock and calendar, and in its largest gesture it can be seen as the marking of the passage of a great deal of time. The very immensity of the cycle, a whole century, is an indictment of the murderous slowness of badly needed change, of the tardiness of salvation's arrival. The playwright, telling the story of Justice arriving for African-Americans, required a century, to our national shame; and to our national shame today, when hard-won progress is being rolled back, the uncertainty, the Maybe and Almost, persists.

Five plays, five decades after *Seven Guitars*, in *Radio Golf*, the grand arc of Wilson's cycle concludes, as the Oedipus Cycle did before it, with the odd spectacle of bloody, unappeasable familial and historical tragedy appeased, not in some gory apocalypse that delivers absolute, unanswerable justice, but by tragedy's safe, undramatic confinement within the sanity of law. No great tragedy, dramatic or historical, is truly resolved. Tragedy cannot be answered; at best, it concludes. To provide that conclusion, reason must be summoned. By reason's introduction, change can happen, progress can actually be made, and tragedy, though unanswerable, can be remediable. Mediated by reason, the world can be repaired and a New Time can begin. The cycle of death can be broken. But even in the New Time, even in paradise, echoes of the past will sound, cries of pain and despair.

Having been made to wait too long, John the Baptist kills his Christ. We mourn that he had in his marrow too little of the divine, and too much of Cain, but we must also forgive him, for being human, like us. A playwright, recording the teleological narrative of his people, traveling from justice delayed and denied toward the light, mustn't avert his eyes from darkness and despair. His hope makes him write, but it can't and mustn't wash the blood away. His job is keeping track of progress and also of the millions miserably slain. He knows, though his 1948 characters cannot, that change (of which, in *Seven Guitars*, Joe Louis is the harbinger) is coming. Perhaps, midway through his tale, he finds the tension unbearable, knowing that the change that *will* come is something for which his characters can only cling to a damaged hope; and in sympathy, in rage, in a synthesis of the two, he stages an apocalypse. If we are saved, we must remember those who weren't. If we are saved, we must remember that it might not have been so. Even when time, oppression and suffering finally end and paradise commences, even after all the dead are resurrected, won't we still need memory, and our close brush with apocalypse, in order to grieve?

Tony Kushner's plays include Angels in America, Homebody/Kabul *and* Caroline, or Change, *which received the 2007 Olivier Award for Best Musical.*

SEVEN GUITARS

1948

Seven Guitars opened on January 21, 1995, at The Goodman Theatre (Robert Falls, Artistic Director; Roche Schulfer, Executive Director) in Chicago. It was directed by Walter Dallas; the set design was by Scott Bradley, the costume design was by Constanza Romero, the lighting design was by Christopher Akerlind, the sound design was by Tom Clark; the musical director was Dwight Andrews, the production stage manager was T. Paul Lynch and the stage manager was Paula Neeley-Wipf. The cast was as follows:

LOUISE	Michele Shay
CANEWELL	Ruben Santiago-Hudson
RED CARTER	Tommy Hollis
VERA	Viola Davis
HEDLEY	Albert Hall
FLOYD BARTON	Jerome Preston-Bates
RUBY	Rosalyn Coleman

Seven Guitars opened on September 15, 1995, at the Huntington Theatre Company (Peter Altman, Producing Director; Michael Masso, Managing Director) in Boston, Massachusetts. It was directed by Lloyd Richards; the set design was by Scott Bradley, the costume design was by Constanza Romero, the lighting design was by Christopher Akerlind, the sound design was by

Tom Clark; the musical director was Dwight Andrews, the production stage manager was Jane E. Neufeld and the stage manager was Narda Alcorn. The cast was as follows:

LOUISE	Michele Shay
CANEWELL	Ruben Santiago-Hudson
RED CARTER	Tommy Hollis
VERA	Viola Davis
HEDLEY	Zakes Mokae
FLOYD BARTON	Keith David
RUBY	Rosalyn Coleman

Seven Guitars had its Broadway premiere at the Walter Kerr Theatre on March 28, 1996. It was directed by Lloyd Richards; the set design was by Scott Bradley, the costume design was by Constanza Romero, the lighting design was by Christopher Akerlind, the sound design was by Tom Clark; the musical director was Dwight Andrews and the production stage manager was Jane E. Neufeld. The cast was as follows:

LOUISE	Michele Shay
CANEWELL	Ruben Santiago-Hudson
RED CARTER	Tommy Hollis
VERA	Viola Davis
HEDLEY	Roger Robinson
FLOYD BARTON	Keith David
RUBY	Rosalyn Coleman

Characters

LOUISE
CANEWELL
RED CARTER
VERA
HEDLEY
FLOYD BARTON
RUBY

Setting

The action of the play takes place in the backyard of a house in Pittsburgh in 1948. It is a brick house with a single window fronting the yard. Access to the room is gained by stairs leading to a small porch on the side of the house. This is Vera's apartment. Louise and Hedley live on the second floor in separate quarters that are accessed by steps leading to a landing and a flight of stairs alongside the building. The stairs are wooden and are in need of repair. The yard is a dirt yard with a small garden area marked off by bricks. A cellar door leads into the basement where Hedley stores his gear. Off to the side and in the back of the yard is a contraption made of bricks, wood and corrugated sheet metal, which is where Hedley kills his chickens and turkeys. It's a primitive mortician table of sorts. There is occasionally a card table set up in the yard with an eclectic mix of chairs. Several light bulbs, rigged by way of extension cords run from Vera's apartment, light the table so they can sit and play cards on the hot muggy summer nights of 1948.

A Note from the Playwright

Despite my interest in history, I have always been more concerned with culture, and while my plays have an overall historical feel, their settings are fictions, and they are peopled with invented characters whose personal histories fit within the historical context in which they live.

I have tried to extract some measure of truth from their lives as they struggle to remain whole in the face of so many things that threaten to pull them asunder. I am not a historian. I happen to think that the content of my mother's life—her myths, her superstitions, her prayers, the contents of her pantry, the smell of her kitchen, the song that escaped from her sometimes parched lips, her thoughtful repose and pregnant laughter—are all worthy of art.

Hence, *Seven Guitars*.

Act One

The lights come up in the yard. Canewell, Vera, Louise, Red Carter and Hedley have gathered in the yard. Dressed in their Sunday best, they have come from the cemetery where they have buried Floyd Barton. There is lingering evidence of food and drink. Louise, in a much-needed affirmation of life, is singing a bawdy song.

LOUISE *(Singing)*:
> Anybody here wanna try my cabbage
> Just step this way
> Anybody here like to try my cabbage
> Just holler Hey . . .

RED CARTER: Hey!

LOUISE *(Singing)*:
> I gave some to the parson
> And he shook with glee

7

He took a collection
And gave it all to me
Anybody here wanna try good cabbage
Just step this way . . .

(A sweet-potato pie sits on the table. Red Carter takes a piece.)

CANEWELL: Uh-huh, put that back, Red! That's my piece!

RED CARTER: How's this yours when I got it?

CANEWELL: I had my eye on that piece.

RED CARTER: You had your eye on it and I had my hand on it.
That go to show you the hand is quicker than the eye.

VERA: There's plenty to go around. Here, Canewell. *(Hands
Canewell a piece of pie)*

RED CARTER: I sure was hungry.

CANEWELL: I didn't eat nothing this morning.

LOUISE: It was hard to eat. I ain't felt like eating nothing either.
But I said, "Let me go on and eat something 'cause I don't
know how long it be before I eat again."

CANEWELL: I want Reverend Thompson to preach my funeral.
He make everything sound pretty.

RED CARTER: I was just thinking the same thing! He almost
make it where you want to die just to have somebody talk
over you like that.

CANEWELL: It sound like he reading from the Bible even when
he ain't. I told myself Floyd would have liked that if he
could have heard it.

VERA: Did you see them angels out there at the cemetery?

RED CARTER: Uh-oh, Vera done saw some angels.

CANEWELL: I saw them out there too. They look like they was
with the funeral home, only they wasn't. Wasn't that them,
Vera? Had on black hats.

VERA: They come down out the sky.

CANEWELL: I seen them. I know who you talking about. One
of them come and ask me how to get to Floyd's house.

RED CARTER: Somebody ask me the same thing. One of them men at the funeral.

CANEWELL: Did he have on a black hat? Look like he was with the funeral home? Had kinda bushy eyebrows?

RED CARTER: Yeah. Had on a black tie.

CANEWELL: That's him. What did you tell him?

RED CARTER: I told him the truth. I didn't know where Floyd was staying at. He was staying in Chicago. Sometime he was staying here. Then he was staying over there. Next time he be staying around the corner somewhere.

CANEWELL: I told him I didn't see where it mattered too much, seeing as how he wasn't home. He just kinda looked at me funny. I believe that's when he went over and started talking to you.

LOUISE: I ain't seen no angels. You all ain't seen none either. Red, did you see any angels out there?

VERA: There was six of them. They come down out the sky.

CANEWELL: They did just kind of show up. Like you looked around and they was standing there. Trying to act like they had been there all the time.

LOUISE: Hey, Hedley, Vera seen some angels at the cemetery.

CANEWELL: Hey, Vera . . . they was all dressed alike? Look like they might have been brothers?

RED CARTER: Maybe they was some of Foster's brothers. If they was with the funeral home.

HEDLEY: I seen them too.

CANEWELL: Hedley seen them. Louise . . . you didn't see them men in black suits always fussing about everything?

LOUISE: They was with the funeral home, fool!

CANEWELL: Naw . . . they wasn't with the funeral home. They *seem* like they was with the funeral home. I don't know who they was. If they was with the funeral home I would have seen them before. They just kinda showed up. Just like you turn around and they was there.

VERA: They carried Floyd away. I seen them.

CANEWELL: When it come time to throw the dirt in the grave, seem like they didn't want nobody to do it but them. They tried to crowd everybody out. I say to myself, "It don't seem right not to throw some dirt in the grave." I figure it was better if I throw it in than if some stranger throw it in. They didn't say anything. I just pushed on past them, scooped up a handful of dirt, and threw it down in the grave. I could hear it when it hit the casket. It was kinda wet and it made a sound when it hit. I say, "You was a good old boy . . . but you dead and gone."

VERA: They carried Floyd right on up in the sky.

RED CARTER: That go to show you I don't know too much about nothing. Because I always swore Floyd was going straight to hell.

CANEWELL: You know . . . I ask myself . . . I wonder did he know.

VERA: The Bible say some things ain't for you to know. It say you know neither the day nor the hour when death come.

CANEWELL: He come like a thief in the night. And he don't go away empty. There's a song what go (*Singing:*)

> He'll come to your house
> He won't stay long
> You look in the bed
> Find your mother gone . . .

Your mother. Sister. Brother. Friend. I don't believe he knew, but then again I do.

RED CARTER: I believe every man knows something, but most times they don't pay attention to it.

VERA: I believe he knew something too.

LOUISE: Whether he did or not ain't done him no good. It ain't made no difference one way or the other. It didn't kill him, but then it ain't kept him here either.

RED CARTER: Hey, Vera, give me a beer.

VERA: I ain't got no beer.

(*Vera starts into the house.*)

CANEWELL: Here, get you a taste of this bourbon. Vera, you
going into the house, put on Floyd's record.

RED CARTER: You can get a whole case of beer for two dollars
and fifty cents.

CANEWELL: I know. You can get any kind you want. Iron City.
Duquesne. Black Label. Red Label. Yellow Label. You can
get any kind of label you want. Some kinds do cost a little
more.

RED CARTER: I would have got a case and carried it up here if
I knew Vera didn't have any.

CANEWELL: I would have carried two. One on each shoulder.
If I didn't have this bourbon. I looked at that bourbon and
forgot all about that beer.

(*The sound of Floyd Barton singing "That's All Right" comes out
of the kitchen window and envelops the yard. There is a moment
of silent reverie.*)

RED CARTER: Floyd "Schoolboy" Barton.

(*The lights fade as the music carries into the next scene.*)

SCENE 2

*The lights come up on Floyd Barton and Vera dancing in the yard of
the house where Vera lives. Floyd is a young man of thirty-five. He is a
blues singer. Vera is eight years younger than Floyd. It is early evening.
They are dancing to Floyd's record "That's All Right," which is playing
on the radio inside the house. A rooster is heard crowing intermittently
throughout the scene.*

FLOYD'S VOICE (*Singing on the radio*):
>You told me, baby, once upon a time
>You said if I would be yours
>You would sure be mine
>But that's all right . . .

FLOYD: Listen . . . Hear that?
VERA: It sound just like you.

(Floyd slides his arm around Vera and begins to dance.)

FLOYD: Come on now . . . you supposed to lean back.

(He bends her back, pushing his pelvis into hers.)

VERA: Come on, Floyd!

FLOYD (*Singing*):
>You told me, baby, once upon a time
>You said if I would be yours
>You would sure be mine
>But that's all right . . .

This is the way you supposed to dance to my record. You supposed to act like you know something about it.

(Vera tries to break away. Floyd holds her closer, singing:)

>But that's all right
>I know you in love with another man
>But that's all right . . .

(Floyd tries to kiss Vera.)

VERA: Floyd, stop it now. Don't be doing all that. *(Breaks away)*

FLOYD: Come here. *(Pulls her to him)* I'll never jump back on you in life.

VERA: I don't want to hear it.

FLOYD: I just say I'll never jump back on you. If you give me a chance I'll prove it to you.

VERA: You done had more than enough chances.

FLOYD: Did you get that letter I sent you?

VERA: What you doing writing me a letter?

FLOYD: I knew that would surprise you. I say, "Vera gonna be surprised to see my name on the envelope." I sure wish I could have seen your face.

VERA: Had somebody writing all them lies.

FLOYD: Didn't it sound good? I like the way that sound. It cost me fifty cents. Some fellow down the workhouse be writing everybody letters. He read it back to me. I say, "Vera ain't never heard me say nothing like this." That be the kind of stuff I want to say but can't think to say. It sounded so good I started to give him an extra quarter. I say, "I'm gonna wait and see what Vera say."

VERA: He ought to have gave you your money back if it depend on what Vera say. I done told you, my feet ain't on backwards.

FLOYD: My feet ain't on backwards either. I just got to missing you so bad. My life got so empty without you.

VERA: Floyd, I don't want to hear that. Just stop it right now.

FLOYD: What? Stop what? I'm telling the truth.

VERA: Go tell it to Pearl Brown.

FLOYD: See, you wanna bring all that up. I told you about all that in the letter. Pearl Brown don't mean nothing to me.

VERA: She sure meant something to you before. She meant enough to you for you to pack up your clothes and drag her to Chicago with you. She meant something to you then. Talking about you gonna send for me when you got up there. Left out of here telling me them lies and had her waiting around the corner.

FLOYD: She wasn't waiting around the corner.

VERA: She may as well have been. She might be waiting around there now for all I know.

FLOYD: Come on now, Vera. You know better than that.

VERA: If you going back to Chicago . . . then just go ahead.

FLOYD: I got to go back. The record company up there waiting on me. They done sent me a letter telling me to come on back. I wanna go back and take you with me. I ain't gonna be here long. I just got to get my guitar out the pawnshop. I might have to pawn my thirty-eight. You still got my thirty-eight, don't you?

VERA: It's in there where you put it. I ain't touched it.

FLOYD: I sat down there doing them ninety days, I told myself it's a good thing I didn't have that with me when they arrested me. Talking about vagrancy . . . If I had that thirty-eight they would have tried to dig a hole and put me under the jail. As it was, they took me down there and charged me with worthlessness. Canewell had five dollars in his pocket and they let him go. Took me down there and give me ninety days.

VERA: Canewell say you threatened to burn down the jail-house. That's why they give you ninety days.

FLOYD: They got that all mixed up. I asked one of the guards to show me the back door in case there was a fire. He said the jailhouse don't burn. I told him give me a gallon of gasoline and I'd prove him wrong. He told the judge I threatened to burn down the jailhouse. The judge ain't even asked me about it. He give me ninety days for worth-lessness. Say Rockefeller worth a million dollars and you ain't worth two cents. Ninety days in the workhouse. (*Takes a letter out of his pocket*) Look here . . . look here. Look what they sent to my sister's house. (*Holds the letter up, brag-ging*) It say, "Come on back to Chicago and make some more records." Say . . . "We'll talk about the details when you get here." (*Vera reaches for the letter*) Naw . . . naw. All you got to know is it say come on back. You ain't got to know all my business. *(Shows her the envelope)* Look at that. "Mr. Floyd Barton." You get a hit record and the white folks call you "Mister." Mister Floyd Barton. *(Hands Vera the letter)* Go on, read it. Read it out loud. "Dear Mr. Barton. Our records show . . ." Go on . . . read it.

VERA *(Reading)*: "Dear Mr. Barton: Our records show you recorded some material for us in August of 1947. We are uncertain of your status. If you are the same Floyd Barton who recorded 'That's All Right' and are still in the business we would like to provide another opportunity for you to record. Stop by when you are in Chicago and we can discuss further arrangements. We are Savoy Records—"

FLOYD AND VERA: "—1115 Federal Avenue in Chicago, Illinois. Sincerely, Wilber H. Gardner, President."

(Vera hands him back the letter.)

VERA: That's nice, Floyd.

FLOYD: I can't go without you.

VERA: I ain't going to no Chicago. You know better than to ask me that. What I want to go up there for?

FLOYD: Wait till you see it. There ain't nothing like it. They got more people than you ever seen. You can't even imagine that many people. Seem like everybody in the world in Chicago. That's the only place for a black man to be. That's where I seen Muddy Waters. I was walking past this club and I heard this music. People was pushing and crowding in the club; seem like the place was busting at the seams. I asked somebody, I say, "Who's that?" They told me, "That's Muddy Waters." I took off my hat. I didn't know you could make music sound like that. That told me say, "The sky's the limit." I told myself say, "I'm gonna play like that one day." I stayed there until they put me out. Mr. T. L. Hall asked me what I wanted to do. I told him I wanted to play at the Hurricane Club. He say he'd fix it.

VERA: I wouldn't put too much faith in whatever Mr. T. L. Hall say. I ain't never known him to do nothing for you. Call himself your manager. What he ever manage?

FLOYD: That's 'cause I didn't have a hit record. It's different now. You get a hit record and you be surprised how everything change. Mr. T. L. Hall done got in touch with Savoy Records to set up another recording date. They waiting on me now. Come here.

(Floyd slides his arms around Vera. She tries to slide away.)

VERA: I told you don't start that.

FLOYD: I want to make you happy. I got something for you.

VERA: It ain't nothing I need. *(Breaks away)*

FLOYD: The first time I ever seen you . . . I never will forget that. You remember that?

VERA: Yeah, I remember.

FLOYD: You was looking so pretty.

VERA: Floyd, don't start that. Ain't no need in you going back through that.

FLOYD: Naw, I was just saying . . . I seen you that first time. You had on that blue dress. I believe it was pink and blue.

VERA: It was two different kinds of blue.

FLOYD: I had just got out the army. They give me forty-seven dollars. Adjustment allowance or something like that. I come on up Logan Street and I seen you. That's why I always say I had a pocketful of money when I met you. I seen you and said, "There go a woman." Whatever else you might say—a pretty woman, a nice woman, a not-so-nice woman—whatever else you might say, you got to put that "woman" part in there. I say, "Floyd, there go a woman." My hands got to itching and seem like I didn't know what to do with them. I put them in my pocket and felt them forty-seven dollars . . . that thirty-eight under my coat . . .

and I got up my nerve to say something to you. You remember that? Seem like that was a long time ago.

VERA: I had just left my mama's house.

FLOYD: I knew you was just getting started. But what you don't know, I was just getting started too. I was ready. You was just what I was looking for.

VERA: You was looking for anything you could find.

FLOYD: I said, "That's the kind of woman a man kill somebody over." Then I see you turn and walk toward the door. I said, "They just gonna have to kill me." That's when I went after you. I said you was just right for me and if I could get that I never would want nothing else. That's why you ought to try me one more time. If you try me one more time, you never carry no regrets.

VERA: I don't carry no regrets now. I'm gonna leave it like that. *(Starts into the house)*

FLOYD: Come on, Vera . . .

VERA: I done been there. Floyd, I ain't going back.

FLOYD: I told you what it was. It wasn't nothing to me. Pearl Brown don't mean nothing to me.

VERA: It wasn't nothing to you but it was something to me. To have you just up and walk out like that. What you think happened to me? Did you ever stop to ask yourself, "I wonder how Vera doing—I wonder how she feel?" I lay here every night in an empty bed. In an empty room. Where? Someplace special? Someplace where you had been? The same room you walked out of? The same bed you turned your back on? You give it up and you want it? What kind of sense does that make?

FLOYD: I told you I could see I was wrong.

VERA: You had what you want and I didn't. That makes you special. You one of them special people who is supposed to have everything just the way they want it.

FLOYD: I see where I was wrong. I told you that. It seemed like she believed in me more.

VERA: You supposed to believe in yourself.

FLOYD: A man that believe in himself still need a woman that believe in him. You can't make life happen without a woman.

VERA: I wanted to be that for you, Floyd. I wanted to know where you was bruised at. So I could be a woman for you. So I could touch you there. So I could spread myself all over you and know that I was a woman. That I could give a man only those things a woman has to give. And he could be satisfied. How much woman you think it make you feel to know you can't satisfy a man?

FLOYD: It ain't about being satisfied.

VERA: So he could say, "Yes, Vera a woman." That's what you say, but you never believed it. You never showed me all those places where you were a man. You went to Pearl Brown and you showed her. I don't know what she did or didn't do, but I looked up and you was back here after I had given you up. After I had walked through an empty house for a year and a half looking for you. After I would lay myself out on that bed and search my body for your fingerprints. "He touched me here. Floyd touched me here and he touched me here and he touched me here and he kissed me here and he gave me here and he took me here and he ain't here he ain't here he ain't here quit looking for him 'cause he ain't here he's there! there! there! there!

FLOYD: Come on. Vera . . . don't do this.

VERA: He's there. In Chicago with another woman, and all I have is a little bit of nothing, a little bit of touching, a little bit of myself left. It ain't even here no more, what you looking for. What you remember. It ain't even here no more.

FLOYD: It's enough for me. It's all I ever wanted. Even if I couldn't see it. That's why I come back. That's why this time I want to take you with me. I told you about all that. I ain't never wanted to hurt you. Whatever you is, that's enough for me. Okay? Now I don't know what else to say. I ain't too good at talking all this out. Come and go to

Chicago with me. I need you real bad. That's all I know to say. I ain't never needed nobody like I need you. I don't want no hit record if I can't have a hit record with you. See? That's all I know to say about Pearl Brown . . . to say about Chicago . . . to say about Vera Dotson. I don't want it if I can't have you with it.

VERA: Then you don't want it.

(*Louise enters, carrying a bag of groceries. There is immediate tension between her and Floyd.*)

FLOYD: Hey, Louise.

LOUISE: How you doing, Floyd? You look like you done gained some weight.

FLOYD: A little bit.

LOUISE: Least they feed you down there in the workhouse. What are you going to cook, Vera?

VERA: Chicken. Potatoes and green beans. And some cornbread. Floyd likes his cornbread.

FLOYD: I can eat a whole pan of cornbread. I like cornbread. I like my chicken too. I can eat two or three chickens.

LOUISE: I can look at you and see that.

VERA: I'll fix you up a plate when I cook it up.

LOUISE: That be nice. That way I won't have to cook. I got a letter from my niece. She got into trouble down there in Alabama and she coming to stay with me. I'll tell you about it.

VERA: What kind of trouble?

LOUISE: Man trouble. What other kind of trouble a young woman get into? Somebody done killed some other body and somebody family done did this or that or the other. My sister say it's best she got out of there. I'll tell you about it. Floyd, I can't wait to beat you at a game of whist. You still play whist?

FLOYD: I done got better.

LOUISE: I done got better too.

(*Louise exits. Floyd puts his arm around Vera.*)

FLOYD: I done got better at everything I do.
VERA: I don't see how, seeing as you ain't had no practice.
FLOYD: Watch.
VERA: Ain't gonna be no watching here.

(*Vera exits into the house as the lights go down on the scene. "That's All Right" comes up on the radio.*)

SCENE 3

The lights come up on the yard the next morning. Hedley enters from the basement, carrying a piece of corrugated tin. He begins to work at setting up a stand where he kills chickens. He makes several trips to the basement. Louise enters from the porch. The rooster crows intermittently throughout the scene.

HEDLEY (*Singing*):
>   I thought I heard Buddy Bolden say,
>   "Here go the money, King,
>   Take it away . . ."

LOUISE: Hey, Hedley. What kind of cigarettes you got? Give me a pack of Old Gold.

(*Hedley doesn't respond. He enters the basement and comes out carrying a crate of live chickens.*)

> Give me some cigarettes. What kind you got?
HEDLEY: Chesterfield.

(Hedley enters the basement and carries out another crate of chickens, which he stacks on the top of the first one.)

LOUISE: I want some Old Gold.

HEDLEY: I told you, woman. Chesterfields.

LOUISE: Why don't you get some Old Gold? You know I smoke Old Gold. Why you wanna be stubborn?

HEDLEY: The people smoke Chesterfield. The people smoke Lucky Strike. The people smoke Pall Mall. The people smoke Camel. Nobody smoke Old Gold. Who you know smoke Old Gold?

LOUISE: I smoke them. There's a whole lot of people smoke Old Gold. Anybody want a good cigarette smoke Old Gold.

HEDLEY: I got Chesterfield.

LOUISE: Give me a pack of them. You seen Floyd? They let him out the workhouse. He come back here talking all that stuff. I hope Vera don't let him back in. He ain't up to no good. She be better off with the iceman . . . as ugly as he is.

HEDLEY: I don't see nobody.

(Hedley takes out a small notebook and writes in it.)

LOUISE: He in there. After three months he liable to be in there all day.

HEDLEY: That's three dollars and forty cents you owe me.

LOUISE: Oh, hush up man. It's liable to be thirty dollars and forty cents before I pay you. You ain't said nothing about paying me for all the biscuits I made you. All them plates of collard greens. Them black-eye peas. Give me a pack of them cigarettes! I got a little book too. You ain't the only one got a little book. I'm going up there and look in my little book and see how much you owe me.

(Hedley hands her a pack of cigarettes.)

HEDLEY: George Butler died. I sell many chicken sandwiches tonight. Many chicken sandwiches. Soon I'm gonna be a big man. You watch.

LOUISE: If you don't pay your rent you gonna be sitting out there on the sidewalk. Talking about being a big man. You gonna be a big man without a roof over your head.

HEDLEY: I always pay my rent, woman. You know that.

LOUISE: You ain't paid it this month. You two days late.

HEDLEY: I pay you tomorrow. Hedley sell plenty plenty chicken sandwiches tonight.

LOUISE: You pay me tomorrow. You know how Bella is about her money. I ain't gonna have her getting on me. And you clean up this yard. I don't want all them chicken feathers around here. And don't you be leaving any of them feet around here either. Did you go down there and see the doctor? You need to go back and see the doctor. You sick. I called them and told them you need to go down there and get tested.

HEDLEY: Hedley not sick no more. I go see Miss Sarah Degree. She give me the root tea. I feel just fine.

LOUISE: You need to go see the doctor. You be spitting up blood. That don't sound like no job for Miss Sarah. You go to see Miss Sarah when you have a cold. You need to go back to that doctor and do what they tell you. They got medicine they can give you. That's what happened to George Butler. He didn't go back to the doctor. You need to get another chest X-ray. Miss Sarah can't do that.

HEDLEY: Miss Sarah a saint. She a saint if ever God made one. She can heal anything. She got a big power. She got her roots. She got her teas. She got her powders. I wonder, do she have a man? Maybe next time I ask her. A woman need a man. That's what Hedley say. I knock on your door last night.

LOUISE: You can knock all you want. You go knock on the doctor's door before you come knocking on mine.

HEDLEY: You know a woman need a man.

LOUISE: I don't need none that bad. I got me a thirty-two-caliber pistol up there. That be all the man I need. You need to go see the doctor. It ain't like it was before. They letting the colored people in the sanitarium now. You can get help. They can make you well. You don't have to die from TB.

HEDLEY: Everybody got a time coming. Nobody can't say that they don't have a time coming. My father have his time. And his father have his time. Hedley is fifty-nine years old. His time come soon enough. I'm not worried about that.

(Canewell enters. He is carrying a goldenseal plant.)

CANEWELL: Who is this out here? Hey, Louise. Hey, Hedley . . . I started to bring my Bible. I'm gonna bring it next time I come.

HEDLEY: "Ethiopia shall stretch forth her wings and every abomination shall be brought low."

CANEWELL: I ain't talking about that. I'm talking about ain't but a hundred and forty-four thousand people going to heaven. That's what it say in Revelations. Say one hundred and forty-four thousand of all the tribes of Israel shall be saved. All the rest gonna be cast into a fiery pit. Next time I'm going to bring my Bible and show you.

LOUISE: Don't you all start that. What you got there?

CANEWELL: This for Vera. This a goldenseal plant. Ask Hedley about them. Hey, Hedley, tell her about the goldenseal. Where's Floyd? Floyd here?

LOUISE: Don't get me to lying. He was out here with Vera. I don't know if he stay the night or not. I hope he didn't. She don't need to be getting tied back up with him. Not after that stuff he pulled.

CANEWELL *(Calls)*: Hey, Floyd! Floyd! Get on out here, man! They got some people from the neighborhood got together and went to see Miss Tillery about her rooster. They asked her to get rid of it 'cause it wake people up in the morning. She told them that's what it's supposed to do. They was still discussing the matter when I come on in here.

LOUISE: She need to get rid of it. This ain't the country, this the city. What she look like with that rooster?

CANEWELL: What you doing, Hedley? You fixing to kill some chickens?

LOUISE: If he start killing them chickens I'm going into the house.

HEDLEY: George Butler died. Hedley sell plenty plenty chicken sandwiches.

(Hedley exits into the house.)

CANEWELL: George Butler died? Every time I look up, somebody's dying. If they ain't dying from one thing they dying from another. I done known six or seven men that got killed. That's why I say I wonder when's my time. Seem like I'm lucky to still be alive.

LOUISE: They be playing Floyd's record more and more. Every time I turn around they be playing it. I got tired of hearing it.

CANEWELL: If he had listened to me he'd be a millionaire by now. *(Calls)* Hey, Floyd! Hey, Schoolboy! I told Floyd if they put the record out it was gonna be a hit. They playing it all over. I told Floyd to get a cut of the money. They paid him a flat rate. I told him not to go for it. If he had listened to me he would be a millionaire by now.

(Floyd comes to the window.)

FLOYD: What you doing all that hollering for?

CANEWELL: Get on out here, man!

FLOYD: I be there in a minute.

LOUISE: I hear you won a raffle down at the Loendi Club.

CANEWELL: I did. That's that radio I give Vera. That's a RCA Victor radio.

LOUISE: I hear you was supposed to win twenty-five dollars with it. Turn some of it loose. I need to buy some groceries.

CANEWELL: Where you hear that? Somebody lying to you.

(Floyd enters from the house. Canewell sizes him up.)

Hey! Floyd "Schoolboy" Barton.

FLOYD: You see they playing the record? I told you! I told you the people would buy the record. I told you! They playing it everywhere.

CANEWELL: I know. I was the one who told you.

FLOYD: Naw. Naw. I knew it was gonna be a hit.

CANEWELL: I did too. I told you if they release it. I didn't know if they was gonna release it or not. I was sitting at home one day about two weeks ago and they played it. The first thing I say was, "I wonder do Floyd know."

FLOYD: Pitts come in the workhouse and told me. "Man, they playing your record." Time I looked around Mr. T. L. Hall was visiting me. All of a sudden he gonna invest some time in me.

CANEWELL: Time? He supposed to be your manager. Tell him to invest some money!

FLOYD: He told me to come down and see him this morning. He going to set everything up. Hey . . . look at this . . . I got a letter from the record company. Come on, we gonna go back up there and make another record. *(Shows Canewell the letter)* You see that? They say, "Come on, we'll work out the details when you get here"!

CANEWELL: I ain't going back up to Chicago.

FLOYD: It's gonna be different this time. We got a hit record.

CANEWELL: *You* got a hit record. You go on with it. I was up there and couldn't get back home. They arrested me for nothing. I ain't going back up there.

FLOYD: You don't have to be in Chicago for them to arrest you for nothing. They arrested me in Pittsburgh. I ain't done nothing but walk down the street. Come home from the cemetery after burying my mama, was walking down the street—and they arrested me. That ain't got nothing to do with Chicago. What's that got to do with Chicago?

CANEWELL: I ain't going back up there.

FLOYD: Mr. T. L. Hall gonna give us the money. It ain't gonna be like before.

CANEWELL: Put me in jail. Couldn't get a job. I don't need all that. I ain't going back up there. They never get me back in the Cook County Jail.

LOUISE: What you went to jail for? You ain't told us all that. You just say you didn't like it. What you went to jail for?

CANEWELL: Nothing. I ain't done nothing. Ask Floyd. Singing. That's all I did. I was right down there on Maxwell Street waiting on Floyd. I started fiddling with my harmonica. I said, "If I'm gonna stand here and play I may as well throw my hat down . . . somebody might put something in it." The police said I was disturbing the peace. Soliciting without a license. Loitering. Resisting arrest and disrespecting the law. They rolled all that together and charged me with laziness and give me thirty days. I ain't going back up there.

LOUISE: I don't blame you. Where's Vera, Floyd?

FLOYD: She in the house getting ready to go to work. Come on, Canewell, go over to the pawnshop with me. I got to see about getting my electric guitar out of pawn.

(*Hedley enters from the basement. Floyd begins to sing:*)

I thought I heard Buddy Bolden say . . .

HEDLEY: What he say?

FLOYD: He said, "Wake up and give me the money."

HEDLEY: Naw. Naw. He say, "Come here. Here go the money."

FLOYD: Well . . . what he give you?

HEDLEY: He give me ashes.

FLOYD: Tell him to give you the money.

HEDLEY: Soon I going to be a big man. You watch. Buddy Bolden give me my father's money I'm going to buy a big plantation. Then the white man not going to tell me what to do.

FLOYD: He ain't gonna tell me what to do either. And I ain't gonna have no plantation. I don't need nothing but that thirty-eight. I was up there in the workhouse. The captain say hurry . . . the sergeant say run. I say if I had my thirty-eight I wouldn't do neither one.

HEDLEY: I gonna be a big man.

LOUISE: You ain't gonna be nothing.

HEDLEY: The Bible say it all will come to straighten out in the end. Every abomination shall be brought low. Everything will fall to a new place. When I get my plantation I'm gonna walk around it. I am going to walk all the way round to see how big it is. I'm gonna be a big man on that day. That is the day I dress up and go walking through the town. That is the day my father forgive me. I tell you this as God is my witness on that great day when all the people are singing as I go by . . . and my plantation is full and ripe . . . and my father is a strong memory . . . on that day . . . the white man not going to tell me what to do no more.

LOUISE: There ain't no plantations in Pittsburgh, fool! This is the city.

HEDLEY: I'm gonna make one.

FLOYD: Hedley say he gonna make him a plantation.

CANEWELL: Hey, Hedley, what you gonna grow?

HEDLEY: I grow anything. Just like the white man. I grow tobacco. I grow oats. Anything.

CANEWELL: You ought to put you in some sugarcane.

HEDLEY: No. No sugar. I hate the sugar. Sugar beat many a man.

CANEWELL: That's how I got my name. My granddaddy used to cut sugarcane in Louisiana. Somebody seen him say, "That boy can cane well." Otherwise my name would be Cottonwell.

HEDLEY: It's gonna be a big plantation.

FLOYD: I just want to come and sit on your front porch and drink mint juleps.

LOUISE: Look at Floyd signifying.

FLOYD: The man say he gonna get him a plantation. I ain't gonna be the one who tell him no. Somebody else gonna have to do that. If I see where he get his that might make me want to get one too.

CANEWELL: You should have heard Hedley night before last, Floyd. He was talking more stuff than a little bit. He was talking about Buddy Bolden . . . Saint John the Divine . . . Saint John the Relevator. Saint Yolanda. Told me his granddaddy was John the Baptist.

HEDLEY: I say he was baptized by a man call himself John the Baptist.

CANEWELL: We was talking about zombies. Lazarus. Hey . . . hey, tell him, Floyd, Jesus ain't had no business raising Lazarus from the dead. If it's God's will, then what he look like undoing it? If it's his father's work, then it's his father's business and he ought to have stayed out of it.

HEDLEY: His father will him to do it. Jesus is the obedient Son of the Father. He was a black man, you know. The Bible say his hair was like lamb's wool and his skin the color of copper. That's 'cause Mary was a Moabite.

CANEWELL: That ain't got nothing to do with Lazarus. What Mary being a Moabite got to do with Lazarus? I'm talking about you ain't supposed to go against nature. Don't care whether you the Son of God or not. Everybody know that. Lazarus even know that. When Lazarus was dying the second time—he was dying from pneumonia—somebody went up and got Jesus. Lazarus saw him coming and said,

"Oh, no, not you again!" See, all Jesus had done by raising him from the dead was to cause him to go through that much more suffering. He was suffering the pain of living. That's why the Bible say you supposed to rejoice when somebody die and cry when they come into the world.

(*Vera enters from the house. She has a man's hat in her hand.*)

VERA: Is you all back on that again? Canewell, you left your hat here.

CANEWELL: I was wondering where my hat was. I thought it might be here. I was too embarrassed to come back and get it.

LOUISE: You ought to be embarrassed the way you all carried on.

FLOYD: What you doing with your hat in my house? You living dangerous.

VERA: It ain't your house. Let's get that straight first. If it's your house, give me twenty-five dollars rent.

CANEWELL: They say wherever you hang your hat is your home. That just go to show you what a lie that is.

FLOYD: That's what I call home. If my hat's there, I'm gonna be there. What your hat doing in my house?

VERA: He left that hat here night before last. Him and Hedley sat out here talking about the Bible and God knows what else. Sat here drinking that moonshine till they passed out. You know how Hedley get.

CANEWELL: I said I was gonna get crazy right with him. Ain't that right, Hedley? We went tit for tat. Hey, Vera, I bought you this goldenseal plant. You plant that over there and that be all the doctor you need. That'll take care of everything you can think of and some you can't. You just take a pinch off of them leaves and make you a tea. Ain't that right, Hedley? Or else get you a little piece of the root.

HEDLEY: You have to plant it now. Don't let the roots dry out. The roots dry out easy.

(Hedley gets a shovel and begins digging in the garden.)

CANEWELL: Tell her, Hedley. That be all the doctor she need.

HEDLEY: My grandmother used to make a tea with the golden-seal. She make a tea or she chew the leaves and rub it on her chest.

LOUISE: We ain't living back when your grandmother was living. You can go right across the street and see the doctor. Dr. Goldblum don't charge but two dollars. You can get some real medicine.

CANEWELL: This is real. Where you think Dr. Goldblum get his medicine from?

(Vera puts the plant into the hole Hedley has dug.)

HEDLEY: Watch you don't plant it too deep.

FLOYD *(Puts his arms around Vera)*: What you planting that for? You ain't gonna be here to see it grow. We going to Chicago.

VERA: I ain't said nothing about going to Chicago.

CANEWELL: You trying to get Vera to go to Chicago and I'm looking to eat my breakfast in a brand-new place.

LOUISE: I thought you was staying up there with Lulu Johnson.

CANEWELL: Naw. I ain't up there no more. I'm drifting right now, but I ain't gonna be drifting long. I get me three rooms and a place to have a little garden and I'll be all right. Three rooms and a woman know how to sit with me in the dark and what else can a man want? If I was Rockefeller I could want for some more money . . . but other than that . . . what else could a poor man want?

LOUISE: Where you staying at if you ain't with Lulu Johnson no more?

CANEWELL: I'm staying down on Clark Street.

VERA: What you got on Clark Street, Canewell?

CANEWELL: Nothing. I ain't got nothing.

VERA: Who you staying with?

CANEWELL: You don't know her. She just some old gal. I'm just helping her out with her rent. We got an understanding about what that is. It ain't nothing. I keep my trunk packed up.

VERA: That's what the problem is now. Everybody keep their trunk packed up. Time you put two and two together and try and come up with four . . . they out the door.

FLOYD: The man said he got an understanding.

CANEWELL: Quite naturally, when it's time for me to go . . . that be the end of our understanding. When it come to the end of our understanding I'm gonna drink a toast and keep on stepping.

FLOYD: Come on, Canewell, I got to go downtown and get my money first. They owe me thirty cents a day for working in the workhouse. That's ninety days' worth of thirty cents. I'm gonna use that to get my guitar out the pawnshop.

VERA: You can go down there and pay on the light bill before they cut it off. And bring something back here if you wanna eat. Even people that have a hit record got to buy some groceries.

HEDLEY: You know why the pawnshop have a sign with three balls? Wherever you see a pawnshop you see them three balls. You ever notice that?

CANEWELL: Yeah . . . come to think of it. They all got three gold balls. Even if it ain't nothing but painted on it. What that mean?

HEDLEY: That mean the pawnshop man betting you three to one you not gonna get your stuff back.

(They all laugh. Floyd exits into the house.)

VERA: How much it cost to go to Chicago?

CANEWELL: It was seventeen dollars and forty cents when me and Floyd went up there. That was last year. They might have put one of them yearly increases on it. Common sense say that can't last but so long if everything go up every year.

(Floyd comes out of the house carrying a guitar.)

FLOYD: Hey, Canewell . . . remember this?

CANEWELL: That's that guitar you got off Odell.

FLOYD: I'm gonna carry this over to the pawnshop and see what he give me for it. Then I wanna go over to the cemetery and visit my mother's grave. Vera, we be back. Joe Louis fighting tonight. Hey, Hedley, Joe Louis fighting tonight.

HEDLEY: The Brown Bomber! Yes! The Mighty Mighty Black Man!

(Vera, Floyd and Canewell exit. Hedley kills a chicken. The lights go down on the scene.)

SCENE 4

The lights come up on the yard. It is several hours later. Vera and Louise are making food preparations.

LOUISE: That's all I know. Ain't no telling what the truth of it is. My sister say it's best if she get away from there for a while.

VERA: When she say she coming?

LOUISE: I got the letter but she didn't say. She didn't say what train or nothing. I pulled that mattress out, I can lay it down on the floor. She ain't gonna be here long, knowing her. With her little fast behind. I believe there's more to it than what they say.

VERA: Probably is. You don't never get the full story.

LOUISE: Talking about love. People don't know what love is. Love be anything they want it to be.

VERA: She might have been in love. Love don't know no age and it don't know no experience. You say she going on twenty-five. She might have been in love. Found somebody treat her half right.

LOUISE: What good it get her? She ain't got none of them now. She lucky she living. Who need that kind of love? One man in the ground and the other in jail. What she got? Went from two to sometime one to none to ducking and dodging bullets . . . for what? For love? No thank you, I don't need me no love. I'm forty-eight going on sixty. Hedley's the closest I want to come to love . . . and you see how far that is.

VERA: Floyd want me to go to Chicago with him.

LOUISE: What for? So he can dog you around some more up there?

VERA: That's what I told him.

LOUISE: You can do better than that. Floyd don't mean nobody no good. He don't mean his own self no good. How he gonna mean you any good?

VERA: I believe Floyd means well. He just don't know how to do. Everything keep slipping out his hands. Seem like he stumble over everything.

LOUISE: However it go he make it go that way. He remind me of Henry. That man walked out on me and that was the best thing that happened to me. When he left I told myself say, "If you have to say hello before you can say good-bye I ain't never got to worry about nobody saying good-bye to me no more." I ain't never going through one of them good-byes again. He was standing upstairs in the hallway. Told me say, "I'm leaving." I asked him, "What for? After twelve years. Why you gonna leave after all this time? After you done used me up." He say, "It's something I got to do." Then he went on and gathered up his things. He left a razor and a pair of shoes. They still up there.

VERA: That's like Floyd left his old guitar.

LOUISE: He got to the doorway and I told him, "Leave your pistol. Don't leave me here by myself." He ain't said nothing. He took out his pistol and handed it to me. I told him say, "I ought to shoot you." We laughed and then he kissed me good-bye. I ain't seen him since. I got that pistol upstairs now. What I'm trying to tell you is, don't let no man use you up and then talk about he gotta go. Shoot him first.

VERA: Sometimes it seems like that more than they deserve.

LOUISE: Maybe you ought to go up to Chicago and find you a man.

VERA: Wouldn't that be something.

LOUISE: If you go up there with Floyd I give him six weeks and he be running around from this one to that one trying to keep you in the middle.

(Floyd and Canewell enter the yard. Floyd is still carrying his old guitar.)

FLOYD: These people around here is crazy. They don't know I ain't going for that. I go down there now the woman see I got the envelope. I ain't got no other piece of paper. She lucky I got that. I got other things to do than keep track of a piece of paper.

VERA: What piece of paper?

FLOYD: What kind of sense that make? She can see on the envelope they done sent me the letter to come down there. They told me that when I was in the workhouse. Say, "When you get out go down there." It ain't said nothing about no piece of paper.

VERA: What piece of paper?

FLOYD: She told me if I didn't have the paper I can't get my money. I told her all that wasn't gonna change nothing. The government still owed me thirty cents a day for my time in the workhouse. I'm the one worked out there in the yard. They wasn't. She told me come back tomorrow.

I'm gonna go down there. Because they gonna give me my money. Paper or no paper, they gonna give me my money.

VERA: What piece of paper?

CANEWELL: When Floyd was in the workhouse they sent him a letter. Say when you get out take this letter down to such and such a place and they will pay you thirty cents for however many days you was incarcerated. Floyd go down there and the woman asked him where the letter was. Floyd ain't had the letter . . . he just had the envelope. She told him they couldn't pay him unless he had the letter.

FLOYD: What kind of sense that make? Paper or no paper, they still owe me the money. Now I got to go back down there tomorrow and straighten that out. I got to wait till tomorrow to get my electric guitar. I needed the money to get the guitar, and now I need the paper to get the money. That's supposed to give you a little starting place. Otherwise they could arrest me right now for vagrancy and give me another thirty days.

(Red Carter enters. He is stylishly dressed.)

RED CARTER: I see you still back up in the alley.

FLOYD: Hey, Red.

LOUISE: Ohh. Just the man I want to see. Give me one of them Old Golds. Hedley give me one of these old Chesterfields. Here, I'll trade you the pack.

RED CARTER: Naw. I ain't gonna do that. I don't want no Chesterfield! I don't see how people smoke them things.

FLOYD: Canewell said he wasn't gonna talk to you. You must have done something to him.

CANEWELL: I ain't said that. How you doing, Red? I said I wasn't going to Chicago with you.

RED CARTER: Who going to Chicago? What Chicago? How you gonna be going with me when I ain't going my damn self? I ain't said nothing about Chicago.

FLOYD: Come on, we going back up and make another record. They sent the letter to my sister's house.

RED CARTER: The record come out . . . I couldn't believe it. They started playing it on the radio. I told myself, "Floyd always did say it was gonna be a hit."

CANEWELL: I did too. I say *if* they released it.

FLOYD: Come on, we going back up there.

RED CARTER: I don't know. Chicago a long way. It take the Greyhound round about fifteen hours. If I wanted to go that far, I may as well visit my mama down in Opelika, Alabama. Down there where the women soft as cotton and sweet as watermelon.

FLOYD: They got some like that up there. They got some like that in Chicago. They got some of the prettiest women a man most ever seen. Come on, let's go back up there and make another hit record!

RED CARTER: They do got some pretty women up in Chicago. All right. Come on, let's go.

LOUISE: Red, you play bid whist? We gonna play some cards after the fight. I'll let you be my partner. I bet we make a good team.

RED CARTER: You never can tell about nothing like that till after you try it.

LOUISE: Ain't that the truth.

VERA: Come on, Louise . . . you gonna show me how you cook greens?

CANEWELL: You don't know how to cook no greens? You get you about three pounds of turnips and about three pounds of mustard. I like to mix them together. Then you get you a big pot. Put some water in it. Cut the stems off the greens and throw that away. Tear the greens up into little pieces. Don't cut them. Some people cut them. That's where you mess up. Put you in a little piece . . . about a quarter-pound of salt pork in there with them. Turn the fire way down real low and let them cook up about six hours. Throw you some red pepper seeds in there first. Cook that up and call me when it get done.

(Vera and Louise exit the yard into Vera's apartment. Red Carter takes out a cigar and hands it to Floyd.)

RED CARTER: Here.

FLOYD: What's that?

RED CARTER: What it look like? That's a cigar. Ain't you supposed to pass out a cigar when you have a baby? WillaMae done had another boy.

FLOYD: You ain't supposed to pass out this cheap-ass stuff.

RED CARTER: Here you go, Canewell.

FLOYD: You supposed to get you some of them dollar cigars.

RED CARTER: Joe Louis' daddy didn't pass out dollar cigars.

CANEWELL: Joe Louis' daddy ain't never seen no dollar cigar. Joe Louis' daddy was a poor man. I know you is too. But damn if they couldn't have been ten-cent cigars. One of them ten-cent King Edwards.

FLOYD: King Edwards don't cost but a nickel.

CANEWELL: I said one of them ten-cent King Edwards. You not listening.

FLOYD: King Edwards don't cost but a nickel.

CANEWELL: That's the kind you know about. But you can buy some King Edward cigars that cost a quarter. Tell him, Red.

RED CARTER: They got some King Edwards cost fifty cents.

FLOYD: This cigar is stale.

RED CARTER: That's 'cause I been carrying it around with me for nine months.

FLOYD: How's WillaMae doing?

RED CARTER: She back at home now. That nine pound twelve ounces took a lot out of her, but she handling it. Seem like he don't never stop eating. If I ate that much I wouldn't be able to get out the house. I wouldn't fit through the doorway. I wouldn't be able to get to the outhouse.

FLOYD: Hey, Canewell, you remember that little rhyme about "in days of old when knights was bold"? I was trying to tell Red one time and couldn't think of it.

CANEWELL:

> In days of old when knights was bold
> And paper wasn't invented
> They wiped their ass on a blade of grass—

FLOYD AND CANEWELL:

> —And walked away contented!

CANEWELL: But do you know this one?

> Ladies and gentlemen I stand before you
> To sit behind you
> To tell you something
> I know nothing about—

FLOYD:

> The admission is free
> You pay at the door
> There's plenty of seats
> You sit on the floor

CANEWELL:

> There's room for ladies
> But only men can go—
> And that's about all I know

FLOYD AND CANEWELL:

> We're gonna discuss the four corners of the round
> table!

FLOYD: That always lay me out.

RED CARTER: Do you know:

> One bright morning in the middle of the night
> Two dead boys got up to fight
> Back to back they faced each other
> Drew their swords and shot each other
> A deaf policeman heard the noise
> And came and killed those two dead boys.

CANEWELL:

> Watermelons sweet and green
> Best watermelons you ever seen
> You eat the meat and pickle the rind
> Save the seed till planting time.

You know how to tell if a watermelon is sweet? You don't thump them. You treat a watermelon just like you do a woman . . . you squeeze them. If they soft they sweet. That's what my daddy told me. I don't know if it's true or not about the watermelon. But I do know a soft woman is sweet. There is some women you just melt right into them. I ain't talking about no fat woman. But I do know something about that. There be more woman there than any one man can handle.

FLOYD: There be a lot of them like that. Hard to handle.

RED CARTER: Where they at? I know how to handle them. I used to have seven women. I tried to keep them separate and give them all a day of the week. But that didn't work. I told one of them, "I'll see you on Tuesday. I got something to do Monday." She say, "Naw, naw . . . I see you Friday night." I told the other one, "I'll see you on Thursday, I got something to do Tuesday." She say, "Naw, naw . . . I'll see you Friday." They all wanted to see me on Friday 'cause I was working. There was a time I couldn't get a woman. I go anywhere near a woman they get up and run. Time I got me a job I couldn't get them off me. Women everywhere. All of a sudden I got right popular . . . except they all wanna see me on Friday. I tried to move my Friday woman over to Sunday, but she got mad. My Sunday woman quit me and my Monday woman wanted to see me on Saturday. I got so confused I say the best thing for me to do was quit my job.

(Someone is heard approaching.)

FLOYD: Who's that?
CANEWELL: Ain't nobody but Hedley.
FLOYD: Hey, Red, watch this.

(Hedley enters. He has been out selling his eggs and chicken sand-wiches. It has been a good day, and his baskets are nearly empty. Floyd starts singing):

I thought I heard Buddy Bolden say . . .

HEDLEY: What he say?
FLOYD: He said, "Wake up and give me the money."
HEDLEY: Naw. He say, "Come here. Here go the money."
FLOYD: What he give you?
HEDLEY: He didn't give me nothing.
CANEWELL: You tell him to give you the money. If he don't give it to you, come and see me I'll cut him for you.
HEDLEY: I'll cut him myself.
RED CARTER: Here go a cigar.
HEDLEY: Yes! My cigar smoke better than your cigar.
RED CARTER: Naw, it don't smoke better than mine. You smoke a good cigar but it don't smoke better than mine.
CANEWELL: Red Carter got a baby boy.
HEDLEY: I hope he grow up and be big and strong like Joe Louis. Maybe one day I too have a son.

CANEWELL: Joe Louis fighting tonight. We gonna listen to it on the radio.

FLOYD: What you name him, Red?

RED CARTER: I ain't had the chance to name him nothing. She named him Mister.

CANEWELL: White folks gonna have a fit with a nigger named Mister. Mr. Mister Carter.

HEDLEY: Yes, the Bible say Ethiopia shall rise up and be made a great kingdom. Marcus Garvey say the black man is a king.

FLOYD: I don't want to hear nothing about no Bible.

RED CARTER: I'm with you, Floyd. If I want to hear that, I'd go to church.

FLOYD: God is in his heaven and he staying there. He must be up there 'cause a lot of things down here he don't know. He must not know about it. If he did, it seem like he would do something about it. Being that he God and everything ain't right in his kingdom. Wouldn't you want everything to be right if you was God? So I figure he don't know about it. That's why I don't want to hear nothing about no Bible. Ethiopia or nothing else.

HEDLEY: The black man is the conquering Lion of Judea, you know. He like Toussaint-Louverture. He is the king! Most people don't know that. Hedley know. He know himself what blood he got. They say, "Hedley, go on, you too serious with that." But Hedley know the white man walk the earth on the black man's back.

RED CARTER: Ain't nobody walking on my back. I ain't gonna let nobody walk on my back.

FLOYD: All I want is you to get out my way. I got somewhere to go. See, everybody can't say that. Some people ain't got nowhere to go. They don't wanna go nowhere. If they wanted to go somewhere they would have been there. Time done got short and it getting shorter every day. The only thing I want you to do is get out my way.

HEDLEY: You watch what Hedley say.

RED CARTER: Where them women go? I thought they was gonna cook something. I ain't had a cooked meal in so long.

FLOYD: What's wrong with that woman you got?

RED CARTER: Her mama ain't taught her to cook. She know how to do everything else, but she can't cook. At first I thought she was lying. I come to find out it was the truth. I told her, "Come here, baby. I'm gonna show you this one time." Told her, "Pay attention." Then I showed her how to make biscuits. That's the only thing she can cook. That's why I'm getting fat. You hungry? We can go down there right now and get some biscuits.

FLOYD: You ought to teach her how to open up a can of beans. I don't want no woman who can't cook. She ain't too much good for me. She might be good for somebody, but much as I like to eat she ain't good for me. That's what got me so mad when they arrested me, 'cause I was gonna miss Vera's cooking. I asked the police say, "I done nothing. What you arresting me for?" He say, "I'm arresting you in advance. You gonna do something." I just look at him and told him, "Well, boss, you right, 'cause if I had my druthers I'd cut you every which way but loose." He just laughed, 'cause he know a black man ain't never had his druthers. They took me down there and beat me with them rubber hoses till I said uncle. I told him say, "If I ever meet you out in the back by the alley one day we gonna have some fun." Give me ninety days for vagrancy.

RED CARTER: One time they arrested me for having too much money. I had more money than the law allowed. Must have . . . 'cause the police arrested me, put me in jail. Told me if I had that much money I must have stole it somewhere.

FLOYD: They got you coming and going. Put me in jail for not having enough money, and put you in jail for having too much money. Ain't no telling what they going to do next. (Floyd takes out his .38) That's why I got this here.

CANEWELL: That ain't gonna do nothing but get you arrested for carrying a loaded weapon.

FLOYD: You allowed to carry a loaded weapon, you just can't hide it. You can carry it in your hand. That's your best bet. See, you can carry it like this here and walk right on by the police. They can't do nothing to you. But even if you be carrying a empty pistol they can take and put you in jail for carrying a concealed weapon.

RED CARTER: Let me see that. That look like one of them thirty-eights.

FLOYD: That's a Smith & Wesson.

RED CARTER (*Looks at gun*): That's it. I used to have one just like that. I give it up for this snub-nose thirty-two.

(*Red Carter takes out his pistol and shows it to Floyd. Hedley exits into the cellar.*)

FLOYD: I'd rather have that thirty-eight. This is nice, but that got a bigger bullet.

CANEWELL: I don't need me nothing but this here. (*Takes out an average-size but thoroughly professional pocket knife*)

RED CARTER: What you gonna do with that?

FLOYD: Canewell cut him some people now. Everybody know that. There's a whole lot of niggers around here wearing Canewell's scars.

RED CARTER: Somebody go to cut me and I be done put four or five holes in him before he can draw back his arm.

CANEWELL: Naw. Naw. It don't work that way. There a lot of people think it work that way. And there a lot of people that used to think it worked that way. Most of them is in the graveyard. The ones that still think that way, that's where they headed.

RED CARTER: That's 'cause they gun wasn't oiled. You keep you gun oiled and your trigger finger strong the only thing can beat you is a bigger or a faster gun. You can't get beat

with no knife. A knife ain't nothing but a piece of history.
It's out of style.

CANEWELL: Cutting don't never go out of style. And you don't
have to depend on nobody for nothing. They quit making
them bullets and ain't nothing you can do but try and beat
somebody over the head with that hunk of metal.

RED CARTER: If you live long enough you just might find out.

(Hedley comes out of the cellar carrying a large butcher knife.)

FLOYD: What that you got?

CANEWELL: Hedley got his chicken knife. He a smart man. If
it be me and him against you all . . . we'd win.

FLOYD: Naw. Naw. Not in nineteen forty-eight. That's why we
won the war. We had bigger guns. You can't fight with knives
no more. They got the atomic bomb and everything.

RED CARTER: You don't need no atomic bomb. That ain't nothing but a big knife. This little thirty-two can handle that.

HEDLEY: But can you handle this? *(Holds up a hot pepper)*

RED CARTER: What's that?

CANEWELL: Hedley got them peppers.

(Hedley pops one into his mouth and offers one to Floyd.)

FLOYD: Naw . . . naw. You never get me to eat that. Give one to
Red Carter. Hey, Red, eat one of them peppers.

RED CARTER: It ain't nothing but a pepper. *(Puts one in his mouth
and almost chokes)*

CANEWELL: Hey, Red, how many fingers I got up? Everything
gonna stay like that for about a week. You ain't gonna see
straight till tomorrow morning.

(Red Carter almost trips over Floyd's guitar.)

FLOYD: Watch it, Red. Watch it!

CANEWELL: Floyd have a fit if you trip over his guitar.

FLOYD: I get my electric guitar. That will make me play better.

CANEWELL: Having a nice guitar don't make you play no better.

FLOYD: Not if you don't know how to play. But if you already know how to play good, a nice guitar will make you feel better about yourself. If you feel better about yourself, quite naturally you be able to play better. People see you with a nice guitar they know you put the music first. Even if you don't put the music first . . . it will work its way to the front. I know. I tried it many a time. I say, "Let me put this music down and leave it alone." Then one day you be walking along and the music jump on you. It just grab hold of you and hang on. Ain't too much you can do then.

CANEWELL: If I could put the music down I would have been a preacher. Many a time I felt God was calling. But the devil was calling too, and it seem like he call louder. God speak in a whisper and the devil shout.

RED CARTER: They say God have planned but the devil have planned also.

FLOYD: Yeah, well, I'm planning too. I get that guitar. Mr. T. L. Hall give me the rest of the money and we be in Chicago making another hit record.

RED CARTER: You supposed to get my drums out the pawn.

FLOYD: Where your drums? I thought you had some drums. They told me you was raising all kind of hell down at the Workmen's Club.

RED CARTER: That's when I had my drums. They in the pawnshop now.

FLOYD: They your drums.

RED CARTER: Tell him, Canewell. They my drums but it's his band. When the record come out it ain't gonna have my name on it. It ain't gonna have your name on it. It's gonna say "Floyd 'Schoolboy' Barton." Just like the other one. If it have your name on it you supposed to take care of the band. Otherwise I don't need my drums. Let them stay in the pawnshop.

CANEWELL: That's right. That where Mr. T. L. Hall come in. Go down there and tell him your drummer need twenty-five dollars to get his drums out the pawnshop. Tell him my harmonica in there too. He supposed to be your manager. You supposed to pass the cost of running the band along to him.

FLOYD: The main thing is to get up to Chicago.

CANEWELL: I'll tell you this up front . . . *if* I go to Chicago. I say . . . *if* I go to Chicago. I want everything up front. It ain't gonna be like the last time. See, bad luck and trouble try and follow me but I don't let it.

FLOYD: You ain't got to worry about nothing. Let me take care of it.

CANEWELL: I ain't gonna let nobody make no fool out of me.

RED CARTER: I ain't gonna let nobody make no fool out of me either. And I know you don't need to hear me say that twice.

FLOYD: That's all in Canewell's head. Ain't nobody making no fool out of him. That's the way the recording business work. You ain't gonna change that. The main thing is to get the record out there. Let the people hear it. Then come back and ask for more money. Then you can get double if it's any good. You can't be good just 'cause you say you is. The people got to hear it and want to buy it. That's what make you good. That's what I was trying to tell you when you walked out.

CANEWELL: I walked out 'cause the man didn't want to pay me what he said he was going to pay me. He didn't want to pay the agreed-upon price. He wanna halfway be in the liquor business. Twenty-five dollars and a bottle of whiskey do not make thirty-five dollars. He walked up and handed me the whiskey. I took it 'cause I thought it was a present. Then he wanna charge me ten dollars for it. That ain't no way to do nobody.

RED CARTER: It ain't gonna work like that with me either. We may as well get this straight now. If he tell me thirty-five dollars, that's what he gonna pay me.

CANEWELL: You see what I'm saying? I asked him say, "Is there any other kind of way we can do this?" He just looked at me. I asked him again. I wanted to be polite like my mama taught me. He told me, "Leave." Just like that, "Leave." Just like you tell a dog, "Sit." I told him, "Bye!"

FLOYD: This time it's gonna be different. We gonna get the money up front.

CANEWELL: It wasn't all about the money. He treat me like he didn't care nothing about me.

FLOYD: He don't have to care nothing about you. You all doing business. He ain't got to like you. Tell him, Red, you got to take advantage of the opportunity. It don't matter if he like you or not. You got to take the opportunity while it's there.

CANEWELL: Just 'cause I was there on an opportunity don't mean he got to treat me bad. He on an opportunity too. You creating an opportunity for him.

FLOYD: The man ain't mistreated you. You all just had a misunderstanding. That could happen with anybody.

CANEWELL: I just say it ain't gonna happen with me no more.

RED CARTER: If he try to do that with both of us he gonna have double trouble.

FLOYD: You all ain't got to worry about that. Let me handle the business, Red. I'll get your drums out the pawnshop. I'll go get some more money from Mr. T. L. Hall.

CANEWELL: That's why I say I don't need nothing but this.

(*He takes out his harmonica and blows a few notes. Floyd plucks the strings of his guitar and starts to tune it. Red Carter takes out some drumsticks and drums on the table. The men begin to play. Hedley exits into the cellar.*)

47

FLOYD: Let's see what we got here. *(Singing:)*

> God don't like it I know
> Better quit drinking shine
> God don't like it I know
> Better quit drinking shine.

(Hedley enters from the cellar with a piece of two-by-four, a hammer, a nail and a piece of chicken wire. He slams the board down and drives the nail in it, disrupting the music.)

(Puzzled) What you doing, Hedley?

HEDLEY: Watch!

(Hedley wraps the wire on the nail.)

CANEWELL: Hedley making him a one-string. He say he know something about music.

FLOYD: What he gonna do with one string? He can't do nothing with one string.

HEDLEY: Watch!

FLOYD: You can't do with that one string what I can do with these six. Even if you can do something, I bet you that it be six times one. I make six times as much music.

HEDLEY: You watch. One string make plenty plenty music. One string make plenty plenty music.

CANEWELL: Look out! Hedley say he make plenty plenty music.

RED CARTER: Go ahead, Hedley. Look out, Floyd!

CANEWELL: I got a dollar on Hedley.

FLOYD: He can't top me with no one string.

CANEWELL: He ain't said he was gonna top you. He just say he make plenty music. You the one say you was gonna top him.

(Hedley finds a rock and puts it under the string to add tension to the wire.)

HEDLEY: Now. When I was a little boy I asked my grandfather where his mother was. He say she was long gone far away. Say when he play this he could hear her pray. I asked him, "How?" He say, "Listen." *(Plucks the string)* I didn't hear her. But I learned it and I used to sit and play and try to hear her. Once. Maybe. Almost.

(Hedley begins to play the instrument. It is a simple tune for a simple instrument: really not much more than a piece of wire vibrating. The men listen hard.)

FLOYD: If I could hear my mother pray again, I believe I'd pray with her. I'd be happy just to hear her voice again. I wouldn't care if she was cussing me out. They say you don't miss your water till your well run dry. If I could hear my mother's voice again I never would say nothing back to her. I wouldn't mind hearing her singing either. She used to do that sometime. Used to sing "Old Ship of Zion." I believe that was her favorite. Though sometime she used to sing "The Lord's Prayer." I can still hear her singing . . . *(Singing:)*

> Our Father
> Which art in heaven
> Hallowed be thy name
> Thy kingdom come
> Thy will be done
> On earth as it is in heaven.
>
> Give us this day our daily bread
> And forgive us our debts
> As we forgive our debtors.
> Lead us not into temptation
> But deliver us from evil,
> For thine is the kingdom

And the power
And the glory
Forever. Amen.

RED CARTER: Where your mother buried at, Floyd? My uncle's out in Greenwood.

FLOYD: That's where she at. She out there in Greenwood. I was out there today. Me and Canewell went out there. They got her buried over in the poor-people part. Took me three hours to find the grave. They let the grass grow all over. I took and pulled up the grass and cleaned off her grave. Said I was gonna get her a marker. And that's what I'm gonna do. Because when I leave this time I ain't planning on coming back. I get her that marker and I won't owe nobody nothing.

CANEWELL: They got everybody buried out there. They got George Butler buried out there. They got Jack Harding buried out there. Ed Weatherby. Uncle Doc and Aunt Lil. Raymond Polk. They got everybody buried out there in the poor section. You go out here and kill somebody, they'll take him out there and bury him. Lightning come along and strike you and they'll take you out there and bury you right beside him. It don't matter what your dispute was. Death come along and say, "Wham! Dispute that!" Death is fairer than life. He got a hundred seventeen men to do his bidding. He like the devil, he ain't never satisfied. The devil got a hundred and seventeen men he want seventeen hundred and one more.

RED CARTER: But he do give you a chance. God don't give you no chances. The devil let you roll the dice. See if you crap out.

VERA: Hey, Floyd! The fight's coming on.

(An Announcer's voice is heard from the radio.)

ANNOUNCER: Good evening, ladies and gentlemen. From Madison Square Garden it's Don Dunphy from ringside, where tonight Joe Louis, the Heavyweight Champion of the World, defends his title . . .

(The lights go down on the scene.)

Scene 5

The lights come up on the yard. The men have gathered closer to the radio so as to hear the fight better. Vera and Louise sit at the table, which is covered with the evidence of food and drink.

ANNOUNCER: Louis sticks out a left—another left—a right to the head—and they tie up on the inside. The referee breaks them apart. Louis has been making good use of the jab. They're in the center of the ring now. Louis sticks out another jab and misses with a left hook. Conn grabs and holds. Conn throws a right to the body and a left to the head. Louis counters with a left hook—sticks out a jab and a right that grazes Conn's head. Conn retreats to the rope and Louis tries to pin him there but Conn punches his way out. Conn fires a hard right to Louis' head. Louis backs up and Conn fires a hard right cross and tries to double on the left. Louis takes a step back, bobs and weaves and works his way on the inside and clinches. That punch hurt Louis. Conn tries to take advantage and fires a left and a right to the head. Louis is holding on as referee Marty Blane breaks them apart.

FLOYD: Louis gonna get him.

ANNOUNCER: Louis misses with a left, misses with a right, Conn with a hard left hook to Louis' head. He really wound up that time. Louis ducks a left and right and fires a right cross to the head. Another right. A right lead catches Conn high on the forehead as both men clinch. Louis back out, throws a left and a hard right that drops Conn to one knee.

HEDLEY: The black man hit hard, you know.

ANNOUNCER: The referee is counting over him. Conn appears to be all right as he takes a count of seven. He's on his feet. The referee wipes off his gloves. They're in mid-ring. Louis fires a left and a right. A hard right a left and a straight right that knocks Conn down! He's flat on his back! His eyes are closed! It's all over! It's all over! Joe Louis has knocked out Billy Conn here in the eighth round!

(The men celebrate. They begin to circle the yard chanting "The Brown Bomber." Red Carter grabs Louise and starts to dance with her. He pulls her into the center of the yard.)

RED CARTER: This is how you do the Joe Louis Victory Walk.

(Red Carter begins to dance. Canewell and Louise imitate him. Canewell stops and watches Red Carter admiringly.)

CANEWELL: Look at Red. Yeah, he know how to do that.

RED CARTER: Come on, Vera, I'll show you this. Then I'll show you the Joe Louis Shuffle. You know how to Jump Back?

VERA: I don't know all them little country dances.

RED CARTER: This dance is done all over the world.

(Canewell begins playing his harmonica.)

Follow me now. Do what I say. *(Puts his hand on his hip)* Come on now. Put your hand back. *(Vera puts her hand on her hip)* Now, just let it roll. You ain't got to worry about rocking it. It'll rock by itself. *(Singing:)*

Jump jump here
Jump jump there
Jump jump jump
Everywhere

Jump back . . . Dooley
Jump back, Dooley, when you really wanna blow
  your top . . .

(He jumps back and rolls his hips in a subtly suggestive way.)

See now, this the way this go . . . Each time you got to do better than me. Better than whoever you dancing with. You got to outdo me. *(Singing:)*

Jump jump here
Jump jump there
Jump jump jump
Everywhere
Jump back . . . Dooley
Jump back, Dooley, when you really wanna blow
  your top . . .

(Vera begins to do the dance. It is suggestive, but she loses herself in the science of it without realizing its full expression. Everyone watches Red Carter and Vera dance. They kick up the dust. Floyd broods. His brooding darkens the stage.)

Go on, shake it out!
LOUISE: Go, Vera! That's right, girl! Shake it!

(She urges Vera on: the matron's counsel. Floyd grabs Vera by the arm and pulls her away.)

FLOYD: Look at Red trying to act like he know something. You can't dance, nigger. You lucky you can walk.
RED CARTER: Yeah. The blind man stood on the road and cried. He couldn't see nothing.
FLOYD: I bet he can see this thirty-eight.
LOUISE: Hey . . . hey . . . you all stop now.

RED CARTER: Stop what? Floyd knows better than to mess with me.

FLOYD: I ain't studying you.

RED CARTER: You got to be able to read to study me.

FLOYD: I can read well enough to read the coroner's report. I know how to read "D.O.A." I can read that.

CANEWELL: Come on, Floyd . . .

LOUISE: You all come on now. You all gonna have to leave if you start all that arguing. I don't allow that around here. Come on, let's play some cards.

(Ruby enters, carrying a small suitcase. She is twenty-five. An uncommon woman, she exudes a sensuality that is electric. Everyone stops to look at her.)

Well, look what the cat done dragged in! Child, how come you ain't let somebody know when you was coming?

RUBY: I did. I sent the letter.

LOUISE: I got the letter last week. It ain't had no day, no time, no nothing. Just "Aunt Louise, I'm coming." I know you can do better than that.

RUBY: I didn't know the time when I sent the letter. I had to wait till after Leroy's funeral. Then I had to wait till I could get the money.

LOUISE: Showing up unannounced on somebody's doorstep like an orphan.

RUBY: I ain't no orphan.

LOUISE: That's her, Vera. That's who I was talking about.

RED CARTER: Do you need some help with your suitcase?

RUBY: I don't need no help. I done carried it this far. I needed some help at the bottom of the hill.

LOUISE: If you had told somebody when you was coming you wouldn't have had that problem.

(Ruby gets a pebble in one of her high heels and stumbles.)

RUBY: Got all these rocks around here.

LOUISE: Look at this old country gal with them fancy shoes complaining about rocks.

RUBY: I ain't country. Don't care where I come from. It's all in how you act, and I know I don't hardly act country. (Sits down and takes off her shoes) That's the longest hill I ever seen. I can't be walking up these hills getting all them muscles in my legs.

CANEWELL: For your information, in case you ain't figured it out yourself, this here is called the Hill District. That one of two things a woman coming into Pittsburgh need to know. The other thing is how to find me. My name is Canewell, and you can find me right down there on Clark Street. That's the same Clark like the candy bar. That's down in what the people call Little Haiti. Just ask anybody where Canewell lives and they will tell you.

RED CARTER: Naw . . . don't pay him no mind. My name Red Carter, but sometimes people just call me Red. You can call me anything you want to. What you say your name was?

RUBY: My name is Ruby. I need me some water.

LOUISE: Go on in the house and get some. There's some in the house.

RUBY: Is it cold?

LOUISE: Go on in there and find out.

RUBY: Where to go?

LOUISE: Up them steps to the third floor. The door on the left. Don't go on the right. That's where Hedley live. Just go on up there.

(Ruby starts up the stairs. Canewell goes after her suitcase.)

CANEWELL: Here . . . I'll help you with this.

(Red Carter grabs hold of the suitcase at the same time as Canewell.)

Watch yourself, Red!

RED CARTER: You watch yourself!

CANEWELL: I was here first!

(The two men stare at each other. Red Carter gradually lets go of the suitcase. Ruby takes the suitcase from Canewell and goes up the stairs.)

LOUISE: Come on, let's play some cards. Let's play some whist. Red, you said you'd be my partner. Come on, Floyd.

(Louise starts to clear the table.)

RED CARTER: Naw, I changed my mind. I'll watch the first one.

LOUISE: Come on, Hedley. You and Floyd play me and Vera. Come on, Vera. Deal the cards.

FLOYD: I'll deal. I don't trust you all. You liable to deal from the bottom of the deck.

VERA: We don't care if you deal. Go on, deal them.

RED CARTER: Where your niece from, Louise?

LOUISE: Birmingham. My whole family is from Birmingham.

FLOYD: You ready, Hedley? Let's show them.

HEDLEY: If you going to play, let's play.

RED CARTER: How long she staying?

LOUISE: I don't know. Knowing her and her little fast behind she ain't gonna be here long.

CANEWELL: Louise, I didn't know you had no nieces.

LOUISE: There's a whole lot of things you don't know.

CANEWELL: I guess you right about that.

LOUISE: We gonna beat you next. You and Red Carter.

FLOYD: Your bid, Louise.

LOUISE: Two.

HEDLEY: Three.

VERA: Four.

FLOYD: Pass.

VERA: Clubs.

(Red Carter sits beside Louise, looking on at her hand.)

FLOYD: Now here's what I don't understand. If I go out there and punch a white man in the mouth, they give me five years even if there ain't no witnesses. Joe Louis beat up a white man in front of a hundred thousand people and they give him a million dollars. Now you explain that to me.

RED CARTER: He got a license and you don't. He's registered with the government and you ain't.

FLOYD: What's trumps?

VERA: Clubs.

FLOYD: Who say it's clubs?

VERA: I do. That's what I bid. You said pass. Where you been? Come to the table.

LOUISE: It don't matter to me what it is. I can play on all of them.

HEDLEY: Whoa! Watch it! Watch it! No talking out your hand!

FLOYD: I just asked what trumps was. I can play on them too.

LOUISE: Floyd ain't got his mind on the game.

VERA: I know.

LOUISE: Vera, you selling Mother's Day flowers this year?

VERA: Yeah, if Floyd get me some crepe paper.

CANEWELL: I'll get you some. What you want . . . red and white?

VERA: Three rolls of red and three rolls of white. And one roll of green tape.

CANEWELL: I'll get it for you tomorrow.

(The rooster crows. The duck quacks.)

FLOYD: If I had me a BB gun I'd shoot that rooster. That be a warning to the duck.

LOUISE: Ain't that the truth. She don't need that rooster. All she got to do is go down to Woolworth's and get her an alarm clock. It don't cost but a dollar and forty-nine cents.

CANEWELL: That's one of them Alabama roosters. See, he fall in love with the way he sound and want to crow about everything. Every time the notion strike him. That don't do nothing but get people confused. That kind of rooster ain't no good for nobody. Best thing you can do is try and make a stew out of him. If you wanna take the time to fuss with it. Then you got your Georgia rooster. It don't know it's a rooster. It thinks it's a dog. It crow every time somebody come around. It don't do nothing but make the bulldog mad 'cause it's trying to put him out of a job. Then you got your Mississippi rooster. He sit up on the roost and roost. The sun even act like it wanna come up, he be right there with it. The sun come up at five, he crow at five-oh-one. Seem like he say, "Let me do this and get it over with so I can get back to roosting." He take his job real serious, but he don't want to be working all day. He say, "I crow once in the morning and twice on Sunday. Let you know when it's time to go to church." That's the only time he crow other than if somebody disturb the hens in the barnyard. That's the way your Mississippi rooster is.

VERA: Canewell, where you get all this stuff from?

CANEWELL: I just know it. I know lots of things. I'll tell you another thing about the rooster. The rooster didn't crow during slavery. He say, "Naw. I ain't gonna be part of nothing like that. I ain't gonna wake nobody up." He didn't start crowing again till after the Emancipation Proclamation. The people got to whooping and hollering so, he say, "Naw, you all ain't gonna leave me out." That's why he crow so loud. If you think I'm lying, go and find you somebody from back in slavery time and ask them if they ever heard the rooster crow.

LOUISE: Come on, Vera. We got them. We got them now.

FLOYD: Canewell talking about that rooster distracted me. He don't know nothing about no Alabama rooster.

CANEWELL: You can tell, he ain't no Mississippi rooster. Mississippi roosters crow at five o'clock. I bet he don't even wake up till about eight.

FLOYD: How you know what time he wake up?

CANEWELL: I can hear him from over where I live.

FLOYD: You can't hear that rooster. I bet you five dollars you can't hear him down there.

CANEWELL: Well, you can't hear him real good, but you can hear him just the same. You know there's a rooster crowing.

VERA: Come on, Floyd . . . play if you gonna play. You holding up the game with that. Don't nobody care where that rooster's from or loud he can crow.

LOUISE: Wherever he from . . . he in Pittsburgh now. This the city. Roosters belong in the country. If they belong anywhere. Miss Tillery need to get rid of that thing.

VERA: Come on, Hedley. It's your turn. Louise played a five.

HEDLEY: The rooster is the king of the barnyard. He like the black man. He king.

FLOYD: They don't have all that in Chicago. You ain't gonna find no rooster living next to you making all that noise in Chicago.

CANEWELL: There's more roosters in Chicago than there is in Pittsburgh. There's more people from the country in Chicago than there is in Pittsburgh.

RED CARTER: You right. There ain't nothing but niggers from Mississippi in Chicago. The Sixty-one highway run straight to Chicago. That Sixty-one highway is the longest highway in the world . . . run straight north to Chicago. That Sixty-one highway wore many a man out. That Sixty-one highway—

CANEWELL: We ain't talking about no highway. We talking about how many roosters they got in Chicago.

RED CARTER: That's what I'm saying. That Sixty-one highway run straight out of Mississippi.

CANEWELL: There's too many people up there for me. I don't see how nobody get to know nobody.

FLOYD: There's more people and there's more things to do. More people mean more opportunity. But, see, you don't know how to take advantage of opportunity. You don't know nothing about that.

CANEWELL: I know I ain't gonna stay up there.

FLOYD: Stay here then! I can get me a harmonica player. They got harmonica players on every corner of Chicago.

CANEWELL: They ain't got none like me. You gonna find that out.

(The rooster crows.)

FLOYD: Stop all that noise!

(Floyd gets up and throws a stone across the fence.)

VERA: Floyd! Don't be throwing nothing over there!

(Hedley suddenly gets up from the table and starts to exit the yard.)

LOUISE: Hedley, sit back down there . . . where you going? Come on and finish this hand.

(Hedley doesn't answer. He exits the yard.)

FLOYD: What's the matter with him?

VERA: You know how he gets. I don't know why you wanna do something to get him agitated.

FLOYD: What I do? I ain't done nothing to nobody. Come on, Canewell, take Hedley's hand. Let's beat them.

(The rooster crows.)

RED CARTER: He do sound like a Alabama rooster.

LOUISE: Where you from, Red?

RED CARTER: I was born in Alabama. I was born in the country. Most people don't know that. They think I was born in the city 'cause I got city ways.

(The rooster squawks, loud, irritated. Ruby enters from upstairs.)

CANEWELL: Hey, Ruby. Come on . . . you play whist? If you don't play no whist, I'll play whatever you play if it ain't nothing but pitty-pat.

RED CARTER: Come on. You can be my partner. Get up, Canewell.

LOUISE: You all leave her alone now. She just got here.

CANEWELL: Do you gamble? I'm looking for a gambling woman.

RUBY: Ain't nobody gonna do no gambling. You have to gamble by yourself.

FLOYD: Here you go, baby. You can have my seat. My name's Floyd. Floyd "Schoolboy" Barton.

RUBY: I don't want to play no cards. I don't see why people play cards noway. You ain't doing nothing but wasting time.

(Hedley enters the yard, carrying the rooster.)

HEDLEY: You want or you don't want, it don't matter. God ain't making no more roosters. It is a thing past. Soon you mark my words when God ain't making no more niggers. They too be a done thing. This here rooster born in the barnyard. He learn to cock his doodle-do. He see the sun, he cry out so the sun don't catch you with your hand up your ass or your dick stuck in your woman. You hear this rooster you know you alive. You be glad to see the sun 'cause there come a time sure enough when you see your last day and this rooster you don't hear no more. *(Takes out a knife and cuts the rooster's throat)* That be for the living. Your black ass be dead like the rooster now. You mark what Hedley say. *(Scatters the blood in a circle)* This rooster too good live for your black asses. *(Throws the rooster on the ground)* Now he good and right for you.

(Hedley exits the yard. Everyone is stunned.)

FLOYD: What he do that for? Hey, Hedley . . . what you kill
the rooster for?

VERA: Come on, leave him alone. He ain't right. Hey, Hedley!
Hey! What you do that for?

(*The lights go down on the scene.*)

ACT TWO

The lights come up on Hedley in the yard. Floyd's record, "That's All Right," plays on the radio in the house. Hedley has turned his table into a grill. He is making sandwiches and wrapping them in wax paper. He places them inside his wire basket, which is filled with hard-boiled eggs, cigarettes and candy bars. He wears a long leather apron. Ruby enters. She watches Hedley for a moment, then crosses and sits on the bench.

HEDLEY *(Singing)*:
> I thought I heard Buddy Bolden say,
> "Soon I be a big man someday . . ."

RUBY: What you got in them baskets? Is them eggs? Let me have one of them eggs.

(Hedley takes an egg out of the basket and gives it to her.)

You ain't got no salt, do you?

(Hedley shakes his head no.)

I don't know what I want no salt for anyway. Salt killed my daddy.

What you kill that rooster for?

HEDLEY: Because nobody want him.

RUBY: I don't understand. He ain't done nothing to nobody. That's just like Leroy. He ain't done nothing to nobody either. Now if it had been a mean old dog that was going around biting everybody, he's liable to live forever. Nobody ain't gonna do nothing to him.

HEDLEY *(Singing)*:
   I thought I heard Buddy Bolden say—

(Ruby gets up, brushes off her backside, and walks around the yard. Hedley watches her with undisguised lust.)

   "Soon I be a big man someday . . ."

RUBY: Can you put them feathers in a mattress? I should have you make me a mattress. Make it soft and low.

HEDLEY: Go on, girl. How he to know it soft and low unless he try it? I can make you anything you want. Just be sure you want it.

RUBY: I need me a mattress.

HEDLEY *(Singing)*:
   I thought I heard Buddy Bolden say—

RUBY: Who is Buddy Bolden?

(Hedley busies himself with his work as he talks.)

HEDLEY: It is who my father name me after. King Buddy Bolden.

RUBY: My mother name me after my grandmother. Grandma Ruby. She say she started to name me after her cousin Bertha. Why you father name you that?

HEDLEY: My father play the trumpet and for him Buddy Bolden was a god. He was in New Orleans with the boats when he make them run back and forth. The trumpet was his first love. He never forgot that night he heard Buddy Bolden play. Sometime he talked about it. He drink his rum, play his trumpet, and if you were lucky that night he would talk about Buddy Bolden. I say lucky 'cause you never see him like that with his face light up and something be driving him from inside and it was a thing he love more than my mother.

That is how he named me King . . . after King Buddy Bolden. It is not a good thing he named me that. (*Pause*) I killed a man once. A black man. I am not sorry I killed him.

RUBY: What you kill him for? Elmore killed Leroy for nothing.

HEDLEY: He would not call me King. He laughed to think a black man could be King. I did not want to lose my name, so I told him to call me the name my father gave me, and he laugh. He would not call me King, and I beat him hard with a stick. That is what cost me my time with a woman. After that I don't tell nobody my name is King. It is a bad thing.

Everybody say Hedley crazy 'cause he black. Because he know the place of the black man is not at the foot of the white man's boot. Maybe it is not all right in my head sometimes. Because I don't like the world. I don't like what I see from the people. The people is too small. I always want to be a big man. Like Jesus Christ was a big man. He was the Son of the Father. I too. I am the son of my father. Maybe Hedley never going to be big like that. But for himself inside . . . that place where you live your own special life . . . I would be happy to be big there. And maybe my child, if it be a boy, he would be big like Moses. I think about that. Somebody have to be the father of the man to lead the black man out of bondage. Marcus Garvey have a father. Maybe if I could not be like Marcus Garvey then I could be the father of someone who would not bow down to the white man. Maybe I could be the father of the Messiah. I am fifty-nine years old and my time is running out. Hedley is looking for a woman to lie down with and make his first baby. Maybe . . . maybe you be that woman for me. Maybe we both be blessed.

RUBY: You old enough to be my father. I ain't hardly thinking about no Messiah. You need to put all that stuff out your mind. You too old to be having any babies anyway.

(Hedley exits into the cellar. Floyd enters.)

FLOYD: Hey, Ruby. How you doing?

(Floyd goes into Vera's. He returns carrying his guitar case.)

Ruby, I thought you'd be gone. Be out looking around the city. See where you at.

RUBY: I know where I'm at. I know I'm in Pittsburgh. I done seen lots of cities before. They may not have been up North, but a city is a city. It don't make no difference.

FLOYD: Sure it do. This is Pittsburgh. This ain't Alabama. Some things you get away with up here you can't get away with down there. I'll show you around. It ain't as good as Chicago, but you be surprised at what you find. Come on, don't worry about nothing . . . I'll tell everybody you my cousin.

RUBY: You gonna buy me a beer?

FLOYD: I'll buy you a beer and anything else you want. Come on.

(Hedley enters with boxes of candy. He glares at Floyd.)

RUBY: Well, I got to change my shoes.

(Ruby exits upstairs.)

FLOYD: Hey, Hedley. Is you feeling better today?
HEDLEY: I feel fine.
FLOYD: Did you wake up on time? That's the question.

(Hedley ignores Floyd's joke.)

HEDLEY: I thought you had something to do. You was in a big rush this morning. I thought you went to the pawnshop to get your electric guitar.
FLOYD: Don't say nothing to me about no guitar. You gonna get me started. I go over there to get my guitar and the man tell me I'm two days late. My ticket expired. It wasn't good but for ninety days. He didn't give me but ten dollars on the guitar and now he want to sell it back to me for fifty dollars. I told him it wasn't gonna work that way. Seeing as how I was in the workhouse all that didn't count. They don't know I ain't going along but so far. Then I'm through with it. When I'm through with it there be more hell to pay than the devil got ways to count. I'm gonna take the pawnshop man this guitar and lay ten dollars on top of that. If he don't want to go along with that I'm gonna see if he go along with my thirty-eight.
HEDLEY: The white man got a big plan. *(Busies himself with his baskets. Singing:)*

> I thought I heard Buddy Bolden say,
> "Here go the money, King take it away."

FLOYD: Broke as I am, I need to have Buddy Bolden bring me some money. I'd take it away. I'd tell him, "Wake up and give me the money."
HEDLEY: No. No. He say, "Come here, here go the money."

FLOYD: That's what I'm talking about. I need to have some-body say that to me. Bad as I need some money, I wouldn't care who it was. Buddy Bolden or anybody else. High John the Conqueror. Yellow Jack. Brer Rabbit. Uncle Ben. It could be anybody.

HEDLEY: It is my father's money. What he sent to me. He come to me in a dream. He say, "Are you my son?" I say, "Yes, Father, I am your son." He say, "I kick you in the mouth?" I say, "Yes, Father, I ask you why you do nothing and you kick me." He say, "Do you forgive me?" I say, "Yes, Father, I forgive you." He say, "I am sorry I died without forgiving you your tongue. I will send Buddy Bolden with some money for you to buy a plantation so the white man not tell you what to do." Then I wait and I wait for a long time. Once Buddy Bolden come and he say, "Come here, here go the money." I go and take it and it all fall like ash. Ashes to ashes and dust to dust. Like that. It all come to nothing.

FLOYD: He coming back. And he gonna give you the money. He got to give it to you. What else he gonna do with it? He gonna give it to you and lay the interest on top of it. You liable to buy two plantations.

(Ruby enters.)

Is you ready? Come on.

(Ruby starts to exit the yard.)

I'm gonna follow you wherever you go.

(Floyd follows after Ruby. Hedley grabs Floyd by the arm with a great sense of urgency.)

HEDLEY: You are like a king! They look at you and they say, "This one . . . this one is the pick of the litter. This one we have to watch. We gonna put a mark on this one. This one we have to crush down like the elephant crush the lion!" You watch your back! The white man got a big plan against you. Don't help him with his plan. He look to knock you down. He say, "That one!" Then they all go after you. You best be careful!

(The lights go down on the scene.)

Scene 2

The lights come up on Vera and Louise in the yard. Vera is making red and white flowers from crepe paper.

LOUISE: Julie gave me that dress. You know that red dress. It's too small for me. You ought to try it on.

VERA: I can't get in that dress.

LOUISE: You ought to try it on. It might fit you. I hate to see it go to waste.

VERA: Maybe it'll fit Ruby.

LOUISE: I'll let her try it on, but she's gonna take her little fast behind out here and get her a job. I ain't gonna be taking care of her. They need anybody down there where you are? She know how to dust.

VERA: I can ask and see.

I might just go on up to Chicago.

LOUISE: You can do what you want to do and I wouldn't be one to try and tell you not to do something. I just know even though it seem like Floyd know how to do the right thing . . . he really don't. Floyd is the kind of man can do the right thing for a little while. But then that little while run out.

VERA: I can always come back. The way he talk about it do make you want to see it. Just to see if it's like he say. Maybe I can be a different person up there.

LOUISE: Wherever you go you got to carry you with you. You ain't gonna all of a sudden be a different person just 'cause you in a different city. You can put that out your head right now.

(Ruby enters. She has a letter in her hand.)

Where you been?

RUBY: I been with Floyd. He took me over on the Northside, then he took me down the Workmen's Club and introduce me to some people. He was telling everybody I was his cousin. One man wanted to take me to Harlem.

VERA: Where's Floyd?

RUBY: He went back over to the pawnshop with Canewell. We went over there this morning and the water line broke. They had the whole street blocked off. The pawnshop was closed. They say they was gonna get it fixed and be open this afternoon.

LOUISE: What's that you got?

RUBY: My mother sent me a letter from Elmore. He had the nerve to write me. I can't stand no jealous man.

LOUISE: All men are jealous. Especially if you make them that way.

RUBY: I ain't done nothing to make him jealous. He was always like that. He was jealous when I met him. He don't know that just make you wanna leave him quicker. He trying to hold on to you and end up driving you away. Elmore started to get mean, so I left him. Everybody seen me and Leroy together and knew I had quit Elmore. I told Leroy Elmore was jealous of him. He say he didn't care. Say he still loved me. Asked me who did I love. I told him the truth. I didn't love neither one of them. They both was nice in their own ways. Then they got into a fight. I tried to tell them Ruby don't belong to nobody and Ruby ain't gonna take but so much of anybody. After the fight I saw Elmore and he asked me where Leroy was. Say he wanted to go make up. I told him Leroy was at the barbershop and he went up there and shot him before Leroy could have a chance to say anything.

The problem with Elmore was he never could get enough of me. He used to tell me he wanted to take it all so nobody else could have me. He wasn't gonna leave none for nobody else to hear him tell it. That make you feel funny to be with a man want to use you up like that.

LOUISE: He don't mean you no good. That's for sure.

VERA: That when they say they got blood in their eyes for you. I tell them, "If you got blood in your eye, then you can't see good." What I want with a blind man?

RUBY: It was never enough for him. We lay down at night. In the morning. In the afternoon. Just stop what you doing . . . if you doing anything. Even that don't be enough. I told him one time say, "Baby, look in the mirror and count that as twice."

LOUISE: You sound like you complaining. You hear this, Vera? Child, I can think of ten women be happy to have a man look at them twice. They get mad if he get tired.

VERA: I'd rather that than to have somebody try to abuse you like that. They ain't loving you, they using you.

RUBY: That's what I'm trying to say.

LOUISE: I wonder what he using now. How much time he get?

RUBY: The judge told him he was gonna throw the book at him. He had the nerve enough to tell me to wait on him. He don't know I'm pregnant.

LOUISE: He ain't the only one don't know. Whose baby is it? Elmore's or Leroy's?

RUBY: I don't know. I got to wait to find out. I hope it's Leroy's.

(*Floyd and Canewell enter the yard.*)

CANEWELL: Hey, Vera, you all can bust out them dresses you all got stuffed in the closets.

FLOYD: We went down to the Blue Goose with Mr. T. L. Hall and he arranged everything for us to play at the Mother's Day dance.

CANEWELL: Told Floyd they was gonna give him an advance tomorrow. Say they was gonna give him half the money up front. And . . . tell them, Floyd!

FLOYD: Ask Canewell—we got a date for the recording studio in Chicago!

CANEWELL: June tenth. At ten o'clock in the morning!

FLOYD: Mr. T. L. Hall showed me the letter he got from the record company. Say, "Be there on June tenth to make some more records." Said they were . . . what they say, Canewell?

CANEWELL: "Enthusiastic."

FLOYD: That's it . . . said they were enthusiastic about the prospect!

VERA: That's nice, Floyd.

FLOYD: Come on, Vera, you got to go up there with me. I ain't going up there by myself. Canewell say he going. You can't say no to a man with a hit record.

CANEWELL: I told Floyd I ain't gonna stay but long enough to make the record. There's too many people up there for me. So many people you can't even walk down the street. I ain't gonna stay but long enough to make the record.

FLOYD: We ain't talking about how long you staying. Nobody care how long you staying.

LOUISE: I can't remember the last time I was down the Blue Goose. Vera, you ought to come down the shop and let me do your hair.

FLOYD: I went over to the gravestone man and ordered my mother a marker for her grave.

CANEWELL: He picked out a real nice one. Got two roses engraved on either side of it. It look real nice.

FLOYD: I give him that twenty-seven dollars plus the five dollars I got for selling my old guitar. He say he would try to have it ready by Mother's Day.

(*Hedley enters the yard with his baskets still half full of cigarette boxes, loose candy bars and a sandwich or two. He is angry. He clutches a letter in his hand.*)

HEDLEY: Hedley don't go nowhere!

(*He flings one of his baskets across the yard. He crosses to Louise and stands in front of her. He slowly balls up the letter and throws it down.*)

Hedley don't go nowhere!
     My father . . . he take care of the horses. He take care of the horses for the shoemaker. He take care of the horses for the baker. He take care of the horses for the doctor! (*Flings the other basket across the yard*) He go hungry . . . with no bread from the baker. He walk with nothing but the tops of his shoes . . . nothing from the shoemaker. He die while he wait for the doctor to come! All his life he taking care for the shoemaker. He taking care for the baker. He taking care for the doctor. He get sick. My mother call for the doctor. Three days later the doctor come. She tell him, "I thought you was the undertaker. He died two days ago." He say, "Can I pray?" She tell him, "No." That's what I tell you: "No." The white man cannot help me! (*Stomps on the letter and grinds it into the sand with his foot*) It is a plot against the black man! Hedley don't go nowhere!

(*He exits up the stairs. Everyone looks at Louise for an explanation. Louise picks up the letter and looks at it.*)

LOUISE: Hedley got TB and don't want to go into the sanitarium. He got this letter from the board of health telling him to be down there on Thursday. I called down there and told them. They want him to come down and get tested.

CANEWELL: They letting colored in the sanitarium now. They got one right up there on Bedford. They moved all the white people out and it's sitting there half empty. They looking to fill it up. He ought to go on and let them take him. He can get well.

VERA: That's what Louise tried to tell him.

LOUISE: He talking all this plot-against-the-black-man stuff. You know how he is.

CANEWELL: Everything is a plot against the black man to Hedley.

FLOYD: Hedley say he don't want to go. He got a right for nobody not to tell him what to do. If it was me I wouldn't go either.

CANEWELL: Least he can get well. Everybody don't always have that choice. He lucky. A whole bunch done died without a chance to get well. He one of the lucky ones. He can choose whether he want to live or die.

FLOYD: Then let him choose! He say he don't trust it. How you gonna trust it for him. He know what the stakes are.

VERA: Hedley don't know he can get well. He don't believe it. Louise tried to tell him. He living too far in the past.

FLOYD: Then let him find out. If he don't know he'll find out. He say the white man can't help him. That's a choice he's making. You can't make it for him. Let him find out the error of his ways. If he don't know the consequences he's gonna find out the truth. Hedley know who he is. He know what he think of himself. And he know what he think of the white man. It might not be what you think but you ain't him. You ain't been where he been. You ain't been . . .

(Hedley enters. He walks quickly down the stairs. He has put on a coat and hat. He quickly exits the yard. Everyone watches him as the lights go down on the scene.)

SCENE 3

The lights come up on the yard. Floyd is in the yard alone, pacing. Canewell enters. Floyd looks at him and continues pacing.

FLOYD: I went over to the pawnshop to meet Mr. T. L. Hall and he didn't show up. I went downtown and ain't nobody seen him. He usually be down there sitting around that hotel. Ain't nobody seen him down there. Didn't he say meet him over at the pawnshop at nine o'clock?

CANEWELL: That's what he said.

FLOYD: I can't be playing around. He got the advance from the Blue Goose. He supposed to give me that and get my guitar out the pawnshop.

CANEWELL: It say on the radio that we gonna be down at the Blue Goose on Sunday.

FLOYD: I can't play down there unless I have my guitar.

CANEWELL: That's what I'm saying. They blasting it all over town that you gonna be down the Blue Goose playing the Mother's Day dance. Say Floyd "Schoolboy" Barton with his hit record "That's All Right" and you ain't even got a guitar.

FLOYD: Mr. T. L. Hall told me say, "Be on time." I was over there five minutes to nine. I can't be playing around. I still got to get Red's drums out the pawn. And you heard me tell the gravestone man I'd be back with the rest of the money.

CANEWELL: Did you look in the Brass Rail by the courthouse? Sometime he be sitting in there with a bunch of other white men. Either that or the Oyster House.

FLOYD: I looked in the Brass Rail. I didn't look in the Oyster House. If I knew where he lived I'd go over to his house.

CANEWELL: They don't like that. They don't like you coming over to their house.

FLOYD: That's what makes me mad. He told me to meet him down there this morning so we could go over the details.

I got to get Vera a dress to wear down the Blue Goose. If she gonna go with me she supposed to look like her man got a hit record.

CANEWELL: Her man got a hit record but he ain't got no hit record money. If you had listened to me . . .

FLOYD: I'm tired of hearing that. It's 'cause of you that I only got one record out. If you hadn't walked out of the recording session I'd have four or five records. I should have kicked your ass for walking out. I still might not have nothing, but I'd have my satisfaction. You always talking about if I had listened to you. What you got?

CANEWELL: I got the same as you . . . but I ain't you. I ain't got my name on a hit record. You supposed to have. You supposed to have the Buick you talking about. You supposed to have that guitar . . . Red Carter's drums and some money in your pocket. You a big man, Floyd. People supposed to treat you like a big man. You go down there and tell Jack Smitty that you ain't playing no Mother's Day dance unless he give you a piece of the pie . . . on top of your fee. And you tell Mr. T. L. Hall you tired of him turning your big money into little money. Tell him to turn your little money into big money and you'll give him the little piece. If he can't take the little piece, tell him don't take nothing. You can't go up to Chicago and be a poor man. A poor man have it rough. I might have to cut me somebody the first day. Vera don't want that.

FLOYD: How you know what Vera want?

CANEWELL: I know Vera longer than you have. I know what kind of woman she is. Vera a quiet woman. Chicago's a noisy city. Anybody can tell you the two don't fit together.

FLOYD: Chicago is what you make it. It got some quiet parts. It got whatever you want. That's why everybody go there. That's why I'm going there. I'm going there to take advantage of the opportunity. I'm gonna put out some more records. I know what will make a hit record. I leave here on the Greyhound and I bet you in one year's time I be back driving a Buick. Might even have a Cadillac. If you come visit me you be able to use my telephone. I'm gonna have everything. Some nice furniture. The white man ain't the only one can have a car and nice furniture. Nice clothes. It take a fool to sit around and don't want nothing. I ain't no fool. It's out there for somebody it may as well be out there for me. If Vera go up there with me and she don't like it, I'll send her back. But at least she will have the chance to see the opportunities.

(Red Carter enters. He has been walking fast.)

RED CARTER: Hey, Floyd.

FLOYD: Hey, Red. *(To Canewell)* Once she see the opportunities she can make up her mind. But I'm gonna make sure she see them.

RED CARTER: I'm on my way back down to my cousin's house. He bought some of that insurance. He's pretty upset about it. There's a whole bunch of people who bought some. They got it in the paper. They say he sold over fifty thousand dollars' worth.

FLOYD: Fifty thousand dollars' worth of what? What insurance? They got what in the paper?

RED CARTER: They got it in there about Mr. T. L. Hall. *(Gradually realizes they don't know)* Mr. T. L. Hall got arrested for selling fake insurance. Say he sold over fifty thousand dollars' worth. Him and a fellow named Robert Gordon. Robert Gordon was selling fake insurance for the Security Mutual something or other.

CANEWELL: No wonder you couldn't find him. Who told you that, Red?

RED CARTER: My cousin bought some. The police was talking to him about it. They got it in the paper. Had his picture and everything. I thought you all knew.

FLOYD (*Quietly*): I had seven ways to go. They cut that down to six. I say, "Let me try one of them six." They cut it down to five. Every time I push . . . they pull. They cut it down to four. I say, "What's the matter? Everything can't go wrong all the time." They cut it down to three. I say, "Three is better than two—I really don't need but one." They cut it down to two. See . . . I am going to Chicago. If I have to buy me a graveyard and kill everybody I see. I am going to Chicago. I don't want to live my life without. Everybody I know live without. I don't want to do that. I want to live with. I don't know what you all think of yourself, but I think I'm supposed to have. Whatever it is. Have something. Have anything. My mama lived and died she ain't had nothing. If it ain't nothing but peace of mind, then let me have that. My mama ain't had two dimes to rub together. And ain't had but one stick. She got to do without the fire. Some kind of warmth in her life. I don't want to live in a cold house. It a cold world, let me have a little shelter from it. That's all I want. Floyd Barton is gonna make his record. Floyd Barton is going to Chicago.

(*Floyd exits the yard.*)

CANEWELL: Floyd! Floyd!

(*Canewell goes to catch Floyd. The lights go down on the scene.*)

SCENE 4

The lights come up on the yard. Red Carter sits with Vera and Louise and Ruby. Vera is making red and white crepe-paper flowers.

RED CARTER: That used to be enough. Get you five pound of cornmeal, a couple of eggs, and some milk—even if it wasn't nothing but powdered milk—and make you a meal. Put that with some beans and rice and what more is there? That used to be enough. It used to be all right to have you a rooster. Once upon a time in America it used to be all right to have a rooster in your yard. Now that done changed. It used to be you could leave your door open. Now you got to bar the roof. Ain't nothing went right since I broke that mirror. That ain't but three years ago. That's what scares me. I got four more years of bad luck. I was down Seefus . . . lost all my money. I was going good too. At one time I had forty dollars. I started to get up and leave but then I was trying to get forty more. Seem like everything broke down. Look over there. You got . . . One. Two. Three. Look there. You got seven birds sitting on that fence. You can count them. They sitting all in a row. If that dog next door start to howling I know something. It sure hurt me to pawn my pistol. I don't feel right without it. There's too many people out there act crazy. Too many people with knives. Ice picks. Meat cleavers and everything else. They had one fellow got in a fight with somebody and pulled a hatchet out from under his coat.

(*Vera crosses to the gate.*)

VERA: They called the dog catcher on Miss Tillery's dog. Say she got to get a license.

LOUISE: He ought to have a license. That's how you know he belong to somebody.

RUBY: All you got to do is watch him and see where he go when he go home. You don't need no license for that.

RED CARTER: You need a license for everything. You need a license to fish in the river. The dog need a license. You need a license to sing on the street. You need a license to sell peanuts. Soon, you mark my words, soon you need a license to walk down the street.

VERA: Hey, Red, what did Floyd say again?

RED CARTER: He say he was going to Chicago to make his record and wasn't nothing gonna stop him. Then he took off. We tried to go with him but he wouldn't let us. I don't know what's taking Canewell so long. He was supposed to go on the Northside while I looked down around by the Eighty-eight. Then we was supposed to meet here.

LOUISE: Vera, you look sleepy.

VERA: I didn't go to bed till quarter to four. I was waiting on Floyd. Time I lay down everything was quiet and still. It stayed that way a long time. Then it started to move a little bit. You could hear the birds flying. They make a noise when they flap they wings. Then they started to sing. I started to get mad till I noticed it was daylight. The whole night passed and I didn't even know it. Floyd never did come.

RED CARTER: Canewell might've found him.

I went and looked all the places I was supposed to. I looked down the Eighty-eight. I looked down Taylor's. I looked down the House of Blues. Joe Burton's Pool Room. I looked all over. I even went up on Herron Avenue by the car barn.

(Canewell enters.)

CANEWELL: I couldn't find him.

VERA: Did you look down Irv's?

CANEWELL: I been all over. I been everywhere. Irv's. Hartzberger's. The Loendi Club. The Aurora Club. The Workmen's Club. I don't know where he could be. You seen him, Red?

RED CARTER: Naw. I looked all the places we said. I couldn't find him.

LOUISE: I can't for the life of me place no Mr. T. L. Hall.

CANEWELL: You don't remember him? Used to go around selling insurance. That's how Floyd met him. Had a black Ford. A black shiny Ford.

RED CARTER: Used to wear a straw hat all the time. I believe he wore a straw hat even in the winter.

LOUISE: I know who you talking about now. Had that old nasty-looking hat. Used to wear it pushed back on his head.

VERA: That's him!

LOUISE: I never would have guessed that he was selling fake insurance.

CANEWELL: That's what the whole idea was . . . he didn't want you to guess it. If you could have guessed, then he couldn't have sold nobody no insurance.

LOUISE: It's a shame the way they do the poor people.

CANEWELL: There's lots of poor people. Mr. T. L. Hall say he didn't want to be one. Selling that fake insurance might have been his only chance not to be poor.

(There is a sudden and loud commotion coming from Miss Tillery's yard. A dog barks. A woman wails. A rooster crows. There is a whole cacophony of barnyard sounds.)

Something done happened. Something got them upset. They don't make noise like that unless they get agitated about something. I'm gonna go see what happened.

RED CARTER: I'll go with you.

(Canewell and Red Carter exit the yard. Vera tries to look over the fence.)

LOUISE: What you see, Vera? What's going on?

VERA: Miss Tillery's kneeling down on the ground. I can't tell what's going on. She just sitting there. There some other people over there.

(Hedley enters the yard singing. He is wearing his business coat. He has his apron wrapped around something.)

HEDLEY *(Singing)*:
>   It's my pussin
>   It's my pussin
>
>   Take off your hand from she
>   Don't touch my pussin at all
>   It's my pussin
>   It's my pussin
>   I say you got no argument
>   For the pussin belong to me
>   It's my pussin . . .

Hey. Womens. It's a good day. Fact of the matter is it's a great day. I go see the black bossman. I go see Joe Roberts, you know. "The one hand wash the other," you know that saying?

LOUISE: Last time I seen you like this you had a pocketful of money.

HEDLEY: You are a smart woman. I always like you because you are a smart woman. Come, let's dance. *(Dances around the yard)* You don't want to dance. Okay. I am soon going to be a big man.

VERA: What you got there?

HEDLEY: Where? Oh, this? When I was a little boy I learn about Toussaint-Louverture in the school. Miss Manning. She say, "Listen, you little black-as-sin niggers, you never each and none of you amount to nothing, you grow up to cut the white man cane and your whole life you never can be nothing as God is my witness, but I will tell you of a black boy who was a man and made the white man run from he blood in the street." Like that, you know. Then she tell us about Toussaint-Louverture. I say I going to be just like that. Everybody say that, you know.

I go home and my daddy he sitting there and he big and black and tired taking care of the white man's horses, and I say, "How come you not like Toussaint-Louverture, why you do nothing?" And he kick me with him boot in my mouth. I shut up that day, you know, and then when Marcus Garvey come he give me back my voice to speak. It was on my father's deathbed, with Death standing there, I say to him, "Father, I sorry about Toussaint-Louverture, Miss Manning say nobody ever amount to nothing and I never did again try. Then Marcus Garvey come and say that it was not true and that she lied and I forgive you kick me and I hope as God is with us now but a short time more that you forgive me my tongue." It was hard to say these things, but I confess my love for my father and Death standing there say, "I already took him a half hour ago." And he cold as a boot, cold as a stone and hard like iron. I cried a river of tears but he was too heavy to float on them. So I dragged him with me these years across an ocean. Then my father come to me in a dream and he say he was sorry he died without forgiving me my tongue and that he would send Buddy Bolden with some money for me to buy a plantation. Then I get the letter from the white man who come to take me away. So I say, "Hedley, be smart, go and see Joe Roberts." We sat and talked man to man. Joe Roberts is a nice man. I told him about Toussaint-Louverture and my father and Joe Roberts smile and he say he had something to give me. And he give to me this.

(He takes out a machete that is wrapped in his burlap apron, crosses over, and sits on his stool.)

Now Hedley ready for the white man when he come to take him away.

(The lights go down on the scene.)

SCENE 5

Lights come up on the yard. Hedley sits on the bench with the machete in his hand. He rocks back and forth chanting.

HEDLEY:

> Ain't no grave . . . can hold my body down
> Ain't no grave can hold my body down
> Ain't no grave . . . can hold my body down.

(He begins to walk around the yard in a circle.)

You think the black man a dog in the dust you can kick when you want? I am not a dog! You think you can throw a bone and I run after it. You think I fetch for you and wag my tail for you. The black man is not a dog! He is the Lion of Judah! He is the mud God make his image from. Ethiopia shall stretch forth her wings! The black man is not a dog! I will stir up the dust around me like the eagle stirreth its nest. Like a hurricane I will come through the house. I will make the roof fall! I will stir up the dust around me to let you know I talk this . . . *(Shoves the machete up into the air)* Ain't no grave can hold my body down.

The black man is not a dog. You think I come when you call. I wag my tail. Look, I stirreth the nest. I am a hurricane to you, when you look at me you will see the house falling on your head. It roof and its shutters and all the windows broken.

(Ruby enters from the stairs.)

RUBY: Hedley, what you doing? What you making all that noise for?

(Hedley looks at Ruby.)

HEDLEY: You think the black man is a dog that I will crawl to you? I am a man, woman. I am the man to father your children. I offer you a kingdom! What you say, I am a blind man? I cast my pearls before swine?

RUBY: Hush all the noise. Be quiet! What's wrong with you?

(She starts toward him.)

HEDLEY: I am not a blind man! I will not crawl for you. I am a warrior. When I am in this dust, my knees buckle from war, not from a woman! I offer you a kingdom . . . the flesh of my flesh, my seven generations . . . and you laugh at me! You laugh at Joe Louis' father! I offer you to be the Lily of the Valley. To be Queen of Sheba. Queen of the black man's kingdom. You think I am a clown. I am the Lion of Judah!

RUBY: Hedley, stop all that.

HEDLEY:

> Satan! I will tear your kingdom down!
> Satan! I will tear your kingdom down!
> Satan! I will tear your kingdom down!

(Ruby goes over and takes the machete from Hedley. She lays it down on the bench. Hedley grabs her and kisses her violently. Hedley is feverish with lust. He tries to find an opening to touch flesh.)

RUBY: Slow down, baby. It's all right. Ruby help you. Here. Ruby help you.

(She lifts her dress and gives herself to him out of recognition of his great need.
> *The lights go down on the scene.)*

SCENE 6

The lights come up on the yard. It is early evening. Floyd is burying something in the garden. He smooths out the dirt with his feet. He has a guitar case and a dress box with him. He calls for Vera to come to the window.

FLOYD: Hey . . . Vera! . . . Vera!

(Vera comes to the window. Floyd holds the guitar up triumphantly.)

VERA *(From window)*: Floyd, where you been? You been gone for two days. Ain't nobody seen you.

(Vera enters. Floyd picks up the guitar to show her.)

FLOYD: Look at this! Look at this! That's the same kind of guitar as Muddy Waters got. Same color and everything . . .

VERA: Floyd, that's brand-new.

FLOYD: Wait till you hear how it sound. We ain't gonna talk about how nice it look till after you hear how it sound. To do that you got to come to the Blue Goose . . . the number-one blues club in Pittsburgh . . . where the one and only Floyd "Schoolboy" Barton is appearing this Sunday . . . one night only . . . Mother's Day . . . courtesy of Savoy Records. Come one, come all, to hear him perform his hit record "That's All Right" along with his new songs and future hits. That ain't all. Wait till you see this here. *(Takes a dress from the box)* Size nine. That's your size.

VERA: Floyd, it's beautiful. I don't believe it. I ain't never had nothing like this.

FLOYD: If you gonna be with Floyd Barton, you got to go down to the Blue Goose looking nice.

VERA: Floyd, where you been? Where you get all this from?

FLOYD: You know better than to ask me where I get anything from. I took a chance. Lots of times in life you taking a chance. Some people say that's all life is. Say, "I'm gonna take a chance on this . . . and I'm gonna take a chance on that . . . and I'm gonna take a chance on the other." And then sometime you be taking your last chance. If you taking your last chance then you done used up your life. I say I'm just getting started and I didn't want to take no chance of not getting back up to Chicago. So yeah, I took a chance. I went out there to pay the gravestone man the rest of the money. He had the gravestone already made up. It's gray marble. It say "Maude Avery Barton." Got two roses. One on each side. It looked so pretty. He say he have it on the grave by Mother's Day. We gonna go out there and see it. I left out of there and went down to the Greyhound bus station. Look here . . . *(Pulls some tickets out of his pocket)* What that say? "Pittsburgh to Chicago." I told the man to write your name on it . . . he said they didn't do that. I took a pencil and wrote it on there myself. *(Shows her the ticket)* Then I made a long-distance phone call . . . cost me three dollars and ten cents. I called Mr. Wilber H. Gardner, president of Savoy Records, and told him I would be there on the tenth of June. Then I called the Delaware Towers Hotel on State Street and told them to get ready their best room for Miss Vera Dotson . . . soon to be Mrs. Floyd Barton. That is . . . if she say yeah.

VERA: I want to say yeah, but what am I saying yeah to? Another heartache? Another time for you to walk out the door with another woman?

FLOYD: You was there too, Vera. You had a hand in whatever it was. Maybe all the times we don't know the effect of what we do. But we cause what happens to us. Sometimes even in little ways we can't see. I went up to Chicago with Pearl Brown 'cause she was willing to believe that I could take her someplace she wanted to go. That I could give her things that she wanted to have. She told me by that . . . it was possible. Even sometimes when you question yourself . . . when you wonder can you really make the music work for you . . . can you find a way to get it out into the world so it can burst in the air and have it mean something to somebody. She didn't know if I could do that. If I could have a hit record. But she was willing to believe it. Maybe it was selfish of her. Maybe she believed for all the wrong reasons. But that gave me a chance to try. So yeah . . . I took it. It wasn't easy. I was scared. But when them red lights came on in that recording studio it was like a bell ringing in the boxing match, and I did it! I reached down inside me and I pulled out whatever was there. I did like my mama told me. I did my best. And I figured nobody could fault me for that. Then when they didn't release the record, Pearl Brown left. She thought she had believed wrong. I don't fault her for that. But I never lost the belief in myself.

Then when they released the record I realized I didn't have nothing but a hit record. I come back to you figuring you couldn't say no to a man who got a hit record. But you did. And that made me see that you wanted more than Pearl Brown. I'm here saying I can give it to you. Try me one more time and I'll never jump back on you in life.

VERA: I got to thinking and I went down to the Greyhound bus station too. (*Hands him a ticket*) Here. See that? What that say? It say, "One way . . . Chicago to Pittsburgh." It's good for one year from date of purchase. I'm gonna put that in my shoe. When we get to Chicago I'm gonna walk around on it. I hope I never have to use it.

FLOYD: Well, that's all right.

(*Floyd and Vera embrace with a renewed spirit of commitment. The lights go down on the scene.*)

SCENE 7

The lights come up on the yard. Louise is dressed for the Blue Goose. She calls up to the window for Vera. She doesn't get a response and goes and sits on the bench. She talks to herself.

LOUISE: I know it don't take all day to get dressed. I'm dressed. Seem like everybody should be dressed. My mother used to tell me I was gonna be late for my own funeral. She might be right. But then I won't have to worry about getting a seat. I don't know if I can take it no more. They about to drive me crazy. The House of Blues, the Blue Goose, the Red Carter, the dead rooster, the this-that-and-the-other, hurry up and sit down and let's dance and give me a drink and what I got? Who ain't don't know where the other one is or went or ain't going or is going and this one's dead and that one's dying and who shot who and who sung what song and give me another drink and here go a dollar and I ain't got a dime and what's the use and who to do and where ain't you been 'cause being all ain't no telling.

(Vera enters.)

And don't you know her and Hedley went to church. I liked to fell out. She say, "Aunt Louise, I'm going to church with Hedley." That child ain't set foot in a church since she was six years old on a Easter Sunday past the time ten years after I had quit going! Then on Thursday they going to the sanitarium. She talked him into going. You know Hedley wouldn't listen to nobody. I tried to talk him into going. You tried to talk him into going. Ain't no telling who else tried to talk him into going. He sit out here with a butcher knife. Sit out here with a machete ranting and raving and carrying on. She come along and he's gonna up and run to the sanitarium. Act like he anxious to get there. I don't understand it.

VERA: Ruby seem like she got a way about her that the men take to.

LOUISE: I wouldn't be surprised if there wasn't something between them. I done seen stranger things. He told me himself. Say he was gonna go down there and get tested. I just looked at him. I asked myself—

(Ruby enters.)

Where's Hedley?

RUBY: He's not here?

LOUISE: I thought you went to church with him.

RUBY: I did. After we got out of church he said he wanted to go see his friend. I stopped by the drugstore and I thought he be here by now.

LOUISE: Who? What friend?

RUBY: I don't know. Just some friend.

LOUISE: He didn't tell you who it was?

RUBY: I didn't ask him. He just said he was gonna go see . . . Bridge, I think his name was.

LOUISE: Jim Breckenridge?

RUBY: Yeah. That sounds like it.

LOUISE: He gone down there to get some of that nasty moonshine. You ought to have brought him back here with you. Man go from church to the moonshine house. Talking about "Ethiopia shall spread forth her wings" and he won't be able to walk up the street.

VERA: He'll be back soon, Louise. Don't worry about him.

RUBY: I talked to him. He said he was gonna go down and get tested.

LOUISE: It ain't gonna do him no good. Not the way he been around here spitting up blood.

RUBY: I just hope he live long enough to see this baby born.

LOUISE: Say what?

RUBY: I'm gonna tell him it's his. He's the only man who ever wanted to give me something. And I want to have that. He wants to be the father of my child and that's what this child needs. I don't know about this Messiah stuff but if it's a boy—and I hope to God it is—I'm gonna name it after him. I'm gonna name him King.

(Canewell enters. He has a newspaper under his arm.)

CANEWELL: Who's this? Wait a minute. Wait a minute. Let me see if I got my knife. I go down to the Blue Goose with you all and I know I'm gonna have to cut three or four people. Good as you all look. Louise, you look like Queen Esther, and Vera look like the Queen of Sheba.

LOUISE: Go on with that stuff, man.

CANEWELL: What's the matter, Ruby, ain't you going?

RUBY *(Ignoring him)*: I got to go get ready. *(Goes into the house)*

VERA: What did the paper say about Miss Tillery's boy?

CANEWELL: "Policeman Foils Robbery." The policeman was standing there getting his shoes shined. He was loafing on the job and ended up being a hero. The mayor liable to give him a medal. *(Reads)* "A robbery at the loan offices of Metro Finance ended in the death of a Hill District man Friday. Williard Ray Tillery, twenty-seven, an unemployed laborer, was shot and killed while fleeing the scene of the crime . . . Police say the suspect fired two shots at Officer Haywood, who returned the fire, striking the suspect in the back." How come the police is the only one who always shoot straight? Everybody else miss. They may as well not even bother to shoot.

VERA: I didn't know Poochie was that young. I thought he was older.

LOUISE: They come and told her Poochie and she commenced to moaning. The Bible say mourn for three days . . . she started her three days right there. She was out there for about eight hours crying, "My Poochie boy. My Poochie boy." She didn't go into the house till the next morning. They had to get her sister to come from Wheeling, West Virginia. She finally talked her into going in. She just kept saying, "My Poochie boy. My Poochie boy."

CANEWELL (*Reads*): "Police are searching for two other men believed to be accomplices, who police say escaped with an undisclosed amount of cash." See, that's another thing. I know how the police do. They shoot the man in the back. Take the money out his hand and put it in their pocket and say, "Oh, the other ones got away with the money. We still looking for them."

LOUISE: That's a shame any mother have to go through that.

CANEWELL: All Poochie wanted to be was a bricklayer.

LOUISE: He laying bricks in hell now.

CANEWELL: He might have went to heaven now. You don't know. The devil don't take everybody you think he ought to. (*Calls*) Floyd! Come on, man!

LOUISE: Let me go up there and see how this child's getting on. Don't you all leave without me.

(*Louise exits upstairs. Vera and Canewell sit in awkward silence.*)

VERA: Canewell, Floyd and me are gonna get married. See if we can make it.

CANEWELL: I always did believe in love. I felt like if you don't believe in love you may as well not believe in nothing. Even love that ain't but halfway is still love. And that don't make it no less 'cause it's only coming one way. If it was two ways it still be the same amount of love. Just like say I loved you and you didn't love me back. I can still say I'm all filled up with love for Vera. I go walking down the street people can see that. They don't know what to call it but they can see something going on. Maybe they see a man who look like he satisfied with life and that make him walk more better. Make him walk like he got a million dollars in his pocket. If I loved you and this time you loved me back . . . I don't see where my love for you can get more bigger than it already was. Unless I walk like I got two million dollars. Sometime people don't count it if you ain't loved back. But I count it all the same.

Some women make their bed up so high don't nobody know how to get to it. I know you ain't like that. You know how to make your bed up high and turn your lamp down low. That's why Floyd don't want to lose you. I think you and Floyd ought to go ahead and see what you all can make of it.

(Louise enters.)

LOUISE: Bella need to fix these steps. She been saying that for the longest time.

(The sound of a rooster crowing is heard from Miss Tillery's.)

VERA: Miss Tillery got her another rooster.
LOUISE: She ought to have gone to Woolworth's and got her an alarm clock.
CANEWELL *(Calls)*: Hey Floyd! . . . Come on! The people is waiting!

(Red Carter enters.)

I called Floyd. I ain't called you. I thought you was setting up the drums.
RED CARTER: That don't take all day. I come by here to see what was keeping you all. The people is starting to come. Where's Floyd?
CANEWELL: He getting ready.

LOUISE: How you doing, Red?

RED CARTER: Who is that calling my name?

LOUISE: Oh, hush up, man. You ought to be able to tell me in the dark.

RED CARTER: I didn't say I couldn't.

VERA: Here, Red, I got you a flower for Mother's Day. What color you need?

RED CARTER: I need a red flower. My mother still living, and even as I know it got to come to the day I wear a white flower . . . I hope it ain't no time soon.

(Vera pins the flower on Red Carter. Floyd enters from the house. He is dressed for performing and carries an electric guitar.)

LOUISE: Ohhhh. You look sharp. Look at him, Vera.

VERA: Don't he look good! I told him I like that suit.

FLOYD: This some Chicago style. I bought this suit in Chicago. Canewell was there with me. I was telling Vera, they got some nice clothes for women up there too.

RED CARTER: They waiting on you down there. I got my drums set up and they got J. D. Lawrence warming up the house.

FLOYD: I ain't in no hurry. Let them wait. They can't do nothing without me. You got your harmonica?

(Canewell takes out his harmonica and blows.)

CANEWELL: The train leaving the station.

FLOYD: Well, all right.

RED CARTER: Where Ruby?

FLOYD: I got to get on now. If she going, she better come on.

CANEWELL *(Calls)*: Hey, Ruby!

(Ruby enters. She is wearing a red dress.)

RUBY: Is these stockings straight?

(Floyd, Canewell and Red Carter look at her and stop dead in their tracks.
The lights fade to black.)

SCENE 8

The lights come up on the yard. Floyd, Vera, Louise and Canewell enter. They have come back from the Blue Goose.

CANEWELL: I didn't know there was gonna be that many peo-ple. People was crowded in everywhere. They was crowded all the way up in the back, into the corners. J. C. had to close the door, and still had people outside trying to get in.

LOUISE: I thought the floor was gonna cave in with all them people. Then Floyd got up on that stage and started play-ing that guitar . . . the people started to hollering and car-rying on and then I thought the roof was gonna cave in. And Canewell . . . I thought that harmonica was going out of style! The way you was blowing on that thing. *(Singing:)*

> That's all right
> I know you're in love with another man
> But that's all right . . .

I see you all tomorrow. Hedley's probably up there sleep. I can't wait to see Red Carter. He got down there and act like he didn't even know me. Wait till I get him straight. I see you all tomorrow. Good night.

VERA: Good night.

FLOYD: I see you tomorrow, Louise.

CANEWELL: Watch your step now.

(Louise exits. Canewell notices the roots of the goldenseal plant are uncovered.)

Whoa! What happened here? Vera, the roots on this plant gonna dry out and rot. You supposed to put them in the ground. This plant gonna die.

(Vera looks at the plant and starts to fix it.)

VERA: Hedley planted it. I don't know how it got like that.
CANEWELL: I'll fix it for you. Where Hedley keep them shovels?
VERA: Somewhere over there.

(Canewell goes over to Hedley's area.)

FLOYD: We'll fix it. You go in the house and get ready. When I was up there singing "Good Rockin' Tonight," what you think I was talking about?
VERA: I hope I ain't got it wrong. I'll be waiting for you. I like that other song too. What you call it—"Sixty Minute Man"?

(She laughs and exits into the house. Canewell has found the shovel and begins to dig in the garden as Vera exits. Floyd turns around just as Canewell unearths a blue handkerchief with $1,200 in tens and twenties. He stoops to pick it up.)

CANEWELL: What is this?
FLOYD: That's mine!

(Floyd tries to snatch it out of Canewell's hand.)

CANEWELL: Look at this! Look at this! This must be Hedley's stash. Everybody says he don't trust no banks. Scared the white man gonna cheat him.
FLOYD: Give it to me. It's mine.

CANEWELL: How this gonna be yours when I found it?

FLOYD: Because I said it is. You ain't got to know nothing else.
I said it's mine you supposed to give it to me.

CANEWELL: Naw, naw. Finders keepers. Didn't you learn that
in kindergarten?

(Floyd tries to wrestle the money away from Canewell.)

FLOYD: Give me my money!

CANEWELL: You can't just take it from me! How you just gonna
take it from me!

FLOYD: I said it's mine.

CANEWELL: I don't care what you said. You can't just take it
from me. I ain't gonna let nobody take nothing from me.

(Floyd pulls his gun on Canewell.)

FLOYD: Give me my money!

(Canewell stares at Floyd in disbelief.)

CANEWELL: Hey, Floyd . . . this is me . . . Canewell.

FLOYD: I don't care who you are. Give me my money!

CANEWELL: How this gonna be yours when—

(Floyd cocks back the hammer.)

FLOYD: Give me my money!

(Canewell suddenly realizes the truth.)

CANEWELL: You and Poochie.

FLOYD: Give me my money!

CANEWELL: Here, Floyd. You got it.

FLOYD: Poochie took a chance. We both took a chance.

CANEWELL: I understand, Floyd. I understand.

(Canewell hands Floyd the money and exits. Floyd counts off some money, puts it in his pocket, and stands exposed in a shaft of light when Hedley enters. He sees Floyd in the yard. He stops and rubs his eyes. He begins to laugh. It is an odd mixture of laughter and tears. He has waited many years for this moment.)

HEDLEY: Buddy . . . you come. You come, Buddy. Oh, how I wait for you. So long I wait for you. I think to myself many times, "Maybe I die before Buddy Bolden bring me my father's money. Maybe I'm not going to be a big man after all. Maybe my father don't forgive me," but I see you have the money. Give it to me.

FLOYD: Get out of here, Hedley. You been drinking that rotgut. Go on in the house.

HEDLEY: But I see I was wrong. I see you have the money. Give me the money, Buddy.

FLOYD: I ain't playing no game now. Go on in the house and go to bed.

HEDLEY: No, Buddy, give me the money. You say, "Come here . . . here go the money." Give it to me. It's my father's money. Give it to me.

FLOYD: Come on now! Watch it! Go on in the house.

(Hedley attempts to take the money from Floyd. Floyd pushes him down to the ground.)

I told you to go on now! *(Helps Hedley get up)* Here. Come on. Go on in the house now. I'll see you tomorrow.

(Hedley gets up and exits into the cellar. Floyd begins to bury the money again. Hedley comes from the cellar carrying the machete. Floyd, hearing him approach, turns, and Hedley severs his wind-pipe with one blow.)

HEDLEY: This time, Buddy . . . you give me the money.

(The lights go down on the scene.)

Scene 9

The lights come up on the yard. "That's All Right" plays on the record player in Vera's apartment. Louise, Canewell, Red Carter and Hedley are in the yard.

RED CARTER: Floyd "Schoolboy" Barton.

LOUISE: Hedley up here going to sleep.

HEDLEY: I'm not sleep, woman.

CANEWELL: Hedley say he resting. When you see him sitting down he thinking about what he gonna do when he get up.

RED CARTER: What the police say, Louise?

LOUISE: They ain't said nothing. They was out here again looking around in the yard this morning. Asking everybody questions.

CANEWELL: They come by my house too. Asking all kinds of questions. At first they was trying to act like I done it. I was glad they got that idea out their head.

LOUISE: They don't know who done it. They still trying to figure it out.

(Ruby enters from the stairs carrying a blanket.)

RUBY: Somebody need to put a light in that bathroom. The bulb done burnt out.
       I want a beer.

RED CARTER: That's what I told Vera. It don't cost but two dollars and fifty cents a case.

(Vera enters from her apartment.)

RUBY: Take me down the street and buy me a beer.

RED CARTER: I'll buy you two beers. And anything else you want. Come on.

VERA: You leaving, Red?

RED CARTER: Yeah, I'm gonna go. I'm gonna take Ruby and buy her a beer.

RUBY *(To Hedley)*: Here, put this on. I'm going down the street with Red. I'll be back.

RED CARTER: Canewell, I'll see you down the House of Blues sometime.

CANEWELL: Not if I see you first.

LOUISE: Hey, Red, come on back and I'll play you some two-hand pinochle.

RED CARTER: I can't play no pinochle.

LOUISE: That's all right, I'll teach you.

RED CARTER: Well, all right. I'll see you, Vera.

(Red Carter and Ruby exit.)

LOUISE: Come on, Vera, I'll help you with the dishes.

(Louise starts into the house.)

VERA: I started walking away from there feeling bad. I turned to look back and Floyd was floating up above the ground. Them six men was holding him up. He come right out the casket just like they laid him in there and was floating up in the air. I could see where they was carrying him. They was all floating up in the sky. I tried to call Floyd's name but wouldn't nothing come out my mouth. Seem like he started to move faster. I say the only thing I can do here is say good-bye. I waved at him and he went on up in the sky.

(Vera and Louise exit. Canewell and Hedley sit and stare at each other. The silence swells.)

CANEWELL (*Singing*):
> I thought I heard Buddy Bolden say . . .

HEDLEY: What he say?
CANEWELL: He say, "Wake up and give me the money."
HEDLEY: Naw. Naw. He say, "Come here, here go the money."
CANEWELL: What he give you?
HEDLEY: He give me this.

(Hedley holds up a handful of crumpled bills. They slip from his fingers and fall to the ground like ashes. Singing:)

> I thought I heard Buddy Bolden say . . .
> I thought I heard Buddy Bolden say . . .
> I thought I heard Buddy Bolden say . . .

(The lights fade to black.)

END OF PLAY

August Wilson

April 27, 1945–October 2, 2005

August Wilson authored *Gem of the Ocean, Joe Turner's Come and Gone, Ma Rainey's Black Bottom, The Piano Lesson, Seven Guitars, Fences, Two Trains Running, Jitney, King Hedley II* and *Radio Golf*. These works explore the heritage and experience of African Americans, decade by decade, over the course of the twentieth century. Mr. Wilson's plays have been produced at regional theaters across the country, on Broadway and throughout the world. In 2003, Mr. Wilson made his professional stage debut in his one-man show *How I Learned What I Learned*.

Mr. Wilson's work garnered many awards, including the Pulitzer Prize for *Fences* (1987) and *The Piano Lesson* (1990); a Tony Award for *Fences*; Great Britain's Olivier Award for *Jitney*; and eight New York Drama Critics Circle awards for *Ma Rainey's Black Bottom, Fences, Joe Turner's Come and Gone, The Piano Lesson, Two Trains Running, Seven Guitars, Jitney* and *Radio Golf*. Additionally, the cast recording of *Ma Rainey's Black Bottom* received a 1985 Grammy Award, and Mr. Wilson received a 1995 Emmy Award nomination for his screenplay adaptation of *The Piano Lesson*. Mr. Wilson's early works include the one-act plays: *The Janitor, Recycle, The Coldest Day of the Year, Malcolm X, The Homecoming* and the musical satire *Black Bart and the Sacred Hills*.

Mr. Wilson received many fellowships and awards, including Rockefeller and Guggenheim fellowships in playwriting, the Whiting Writers Award and the 2003 Heinz Award. He was awarded a 1999 National Humanities Medal by the President of the United States, and received numerous honorary degrees from colleges and universities, as well as the only high school diploma ever issued by the Carnegie Library of Pittsburgh.

He was an alumnus of New Dramatists, a member of the American Academy of Arts and Sciences, a 1995 inductee into the American Academy of Arts and Letters, and on October 16, 2005, Broadway renamed the theater located at 245 West 52nd Street: The August Wilson Theatre. In 2007, he was posthumously inducted into the Theater Hall of Fame.

Mr. Wilson was born and raised in the Hill District of Pittsburgh, and lived in Seattle at the time of his death. He is survived by two daughters, Sakina Ansari and Azula Carmen Wilson, and his wife, costume designer Constanza Romero.